THE
MUSHROOM
COOK BOOK

ALSO BY GARIBALDI M. LAPOLLA

Italian Cooking for the American Kitchen

THE
MUSHROOM
COOK BOOK

GARIBALDI M. LAPOLLA

Illustrated by the Author

AVENEL BOOKS • NEW YORK

By Way of Understanding the Mushroom

THE MUSHROOM is a plant without leaves, without blossoms, without fruit. It has been with us ever since trees, woods, mountainsides, and fields have been. Some mushrooms are tiny; others are as large as soccer balls. Mushrooms come in shapes like bells, like umbrellas, like twisted little castles, like tall, willowy towers, and sometimes in forms more abstract than Picasso could conceive. Their colors, too, range from oyster white through the subtlest grays to flamboyant oranges and reds, in addition to the tasty familiar cultivated mushrooms which we all buy and eat with such relish. Not only are they so delicious to eat, they are beautiful to look at.

Those sudden growths—sometimes scattered all through woodlands and meadows—once were thought to have been the manna which the Israelites found on their long trek to the Land of Milk and Honey. Actually, that food was probably only a lichen blown in by the winds which, laden with moisture, are compelled as they cross the hot desert sands to drop the little lichen plants to the ground. Overnight they spring up all over the desert, and they are edible as long as they are eaten the same day they are dropped. This phenomenon occurs even today in the deserts around Palestine and in our own Western deserts.

Despite the mistaken notion that it was a gift sent by God to the long-tramping Hebrews of ancient times, the mushroom was looked upon with suspicion throughout the Middle Ages. People considered them strictly inedible and feared even to touch them. Those were the days when the toadstool—or the mushroom—was thought to be the haunt of night creatures, most of whom were bent on mischief to human beings. A sixteenth-century Swiss condemned all mushrooms as unfit to be eaten by human beings or by pigs. And as short a time ago as Shakespeare's day, a cook book writer declared: "There be two kinds of musherons, one that sleeth, and one that doth not."

Happily such nonsense is long past. All civilized cooks know that mushrooms are not only good to eat but have learned by experience that cultivated ones are superior in size and flavor and are dependable. Moreover, cultivated mushrooms are so widely available, so promptly distributed that freshness is assured and no one need take the risk of choosing which of the wild varieties are safe to eat.

As a matter of fact, most mushrooms are not poisonous. They have been eaten by mankind for thousands of years. They were known to the Chaldeans of Biblical times, regarded as special delicacies for the best of tables. Like their modern brothers, the ancient Chinese, the Indians, and the Japanese used mushrooms freshly gathered from the woods and fields. And they learned the art of drying mushrooms whole and of preserving them in the form of a powder, always making them integral parts of delightful dishes. In Siberia, mushrooms are not only consumed as food as elsewhere but they are used to concoct an intoxicating beverage, said to be the equal of our gin and cordials. Among all people from time immemorial, mushrooms have been used as drugs in special diseases and often to combat bacterial infection.

But it remained for the Romans to make a fetish of them. For many years during the fabulous decades of the empire, mushrooms were a rage—even more so than the present vogue for "dry, *but dry,* Martinis." They were so prized that their preparation became inordinately important—with two results: one, that slaves, charged with gathering mushrooms, were flogged if they failed to turn in the whole yield they had gathered. The other was the development of a complete new set of cooking vessels, designed expressly for mushrooms. A poet of the time has a mushroom vessel bemoan its reduction to the level of the meanest slave since it had been used for . . . Brussels sprouts!

The ingenious Americans, however, were the first to capture the volatile spores of a prolific type—the *Agaricus campestris*—and make them yield ever fresh and ever safe mushrooms. It has developed into such a growing industry that now a number of areas in the country boast centers of mushroom growing from which distribution is quick, easy and efficient, while canned and frozen mushrooms are also widely offered in shops and supermarkets. One should be an expert botanist— or to put it more exactly, a mycologist (mushroom specialist) a woodsman or a country man who knows his stuff in order to collect mushrooms in the wild with assurance. Rare is the

person who would risk his remaining days for the taste, texture and the aroma of a mushroom uprooted from the soil and thrown into the skillet before the sun goes down. There is no sure way of knowing that the wild mushrooms you can have for the picking are not poisonous; unless you are an absolute expert on wild mushrooms, stick to cultivated, canned, or dried mushrooms. Discard the old notion that a piece of silver or a silver spoon or a whole clove of clean, white garlic can tell you if it discolors while cooking with the mushrooms that they are not edible. There is simply no basis for believing this. It is a superstition.

But it is a mistake to believe that the delicacy, the delight, the dainty individual flavor of the mushroom cannot be had with perfect and utter safety. First, there are the dried mushrooms that come to this country from all corners of the globe—France, Italy, Czechoslovakia, Poland, China, Japan. There are even our own dried mushrooms—mushrooms found in the forests and the plains of Minnesota, Wisconsin, and of New York—not to mention those of Canada. The dried mushrooms retain the unmistakable scent of their original habitat—a scent compounded of the smell of woods and plain, of mountain and field. Second, there are the canned mushrooms that have found a popular place on the shelves of practically every grocery in the country. These mushrooms are, for the most part, the button type of wild mushroom of the field which we all know so well. They come whole, in caps alone, or in broken but perfectly usable pieces. All are pre-cooked and safe to eat. We also have imported and domestic mushrooms put up in oil or vinegar or both, and of distinctive value on any table.

Last, but by no means least, are the cultivated mushrooms that we see so often—and almost the whole year round—on the counters of our fruit and vegetable shops. It is these mushrooms which most American cooks employ. They are served, however, in only a limited number of ways. This is so since the modern use of mushrooms is recent, at least among the masses of our people. But mushrooms seem to be gaining so in popularity that the imaginative cook has been able to call upon them to serve in many capacities—as snacks, as entrées, as additions to a main dish. Gone is the day when the mushroom was considered a mere condiment. And gone is the day when the mushroom appeared only on the tables of princes and magnates.

Actually the mushroom is a tasty food. Eaten alone, with a minimum of fixings, it is a good choice for persons on slimming diets. Eaten with accompaniments of meat, fish, vegetables, nuts, it becomes a complete and wholesome meal. It is plentifully supplied with minerals and contains a fair amount of vegetable protein and of most essential vitamins.

In this book I have put the emphasis on the cultivated mushrooms, developed from the *Agaricus campestris* of the fields or, as it is called in France, the *champignon*. I have done so because they are so easy to come by, and well within the capacity of most purses. I have not dealt at all with the fresh wild variety. That I must leave to those expert souls who know a safe wild mushroom when they see one. I stress the mushroom grown under controlled conditions not only because of the reasons I have already stated but also because it is safe, it has its own distinctions, and it can make a brave show by itself on any table. At the same time, there is no reason in the world why the dried or canned mushroom may not be substituted for the fresh one. (See further on page 15.)

One word more about the dry mushrooms may not be amiss. The mushroom that is dried in Europe is generally the *Boletus edulis*. It has a remarkable ability to retain its unusual aroma. This goes too for the several other types that are procurable here: the black mushroom of China, the cantrelles, the morels, and the lactarias. These may be only names to you, but they soon can become associated in your memory with distinctive flavors. Often they impart to a sauce or a dish a quality that at

once lifts it out of the commonplace and transforms it into a gourmet's miracle—and all without adding an extra calorie or interfering in any way with the perfect digestion that should always follow a satisfied appetite.

Furthermore, a small amount of the dried mushrooms can be helpful in adding to the delight of the fresh mushroom. One half ounce of the dried to one pound of the fresh mushrooms will perform wonders. That is not to say that the humble *Agaricus campestris* cannot shine forth in its own regalia—it can; often it should; most often it will. But it is possible, by a judicious measurement, to contrive a new flavor with a touch of the *Boletus edulis* or the equally aromatic lactarias. It will make no difference whether you use the sliced forms or the stems or the caps or the whole mushroom. The dried ones come in all these guises. It is generally best to sauté the dried slices or caps before adding them to fresh mushrooms.

Nor are the dried forms difficult to use. Observe the simple rule that you *first* wash them in lukewarm water and *then* soak them in hot. There are authorities who suggest soaking them overnight in cold water. I have found, however, that the Chinese method is best and quickest. The Chinese cooks wash the mushrooms under lukewarm water and then let them stand in almost boiling water for 30 minutes at the most. For the dried sliced mushrooms, 20 minutes will suffice. After that, pat them as dry as you can, preserving them whole, cutting them coarsely, or mincing them as the case may be. Their traditional role is in soups and sauces—in other words, they are condiments and not used as a vegetable, as fresh mushrooms so often are, but employed for their seasoning value.

The canned mushrooms are more limited in scope but can easily substitute completely for the fresh, 6 to 8 ounces of the canned equalling a pound of the latter. Like the fresh mushrooms, they can be a full dish by themselves, a vegetable accompaniment to another dish, or the additional flavor that "makes" a sauce or a soup. But in all cases, just as in the case of the cultivated fresh mushrooms, introducing a small portion of the dried forms often lends that subtle aroma that makes all the difference between the "family dish" and the "guest dish." And I believe in making every "family dish" into a "guest" one!

One word about truffles—a monarch's dish. They are members of another group of fungi. They grow wild underground and cannot be cultivated—the best of them being obtained in France and in upper Italy. A regular industry flourishes to root them out of the ground by means of trained dogs and pigs. The animals smell out the tubers and then dig them up. The pigs, however, are likely to eat the truffles and have to be caught in the act of pulling them out and gently made to part with them. Therefore the great cost of truffles. Cooked in wine, cognac, or champagne, they may be delectable and undoubtedly an extravagance. For the most part truffles are used because of the all-pervading odor they literally pour into foods with which they come in contact. They are best used sparingly and, generally to serve as a flavoring and as an ornament in foods— foies gras, pates, galantines, terrines, and sliced and inserted under the skin of turkeys and chickens.

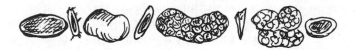

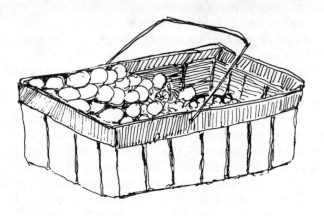

Buying Mushrooms

FRESH MUSHROOMS come into the markets practically throughout the entire year, but especially during cold seasons when they keep much better without being put under refrigeration. How does one know when they are good to buy? Price may have something to do with the problem, but not much. The smaller the mushroom, generally the smaller the price. I prefer the small type for many dishes, but the larger forms are especially good in sauces and in stews.

Quality is more important than price or size. How does one know mushrooms of good quality—of course, it is understood that we are talking of the cultivated—from those of an inferior grade? Naturally, freshness is one consideration. First, the cultivated mushroom, if it is really of the best quality, should be almost a pure white, really an oyster white. It should look clean and have a clean, woodsy smell. Second, the cap, the gills, the stem should be close together—that is, if the cap seems to have broken away from the stem so as to expose the gills, you should reject the mushrooms. You should reject them also if they show too much evidence of oxidation—that is, discoloring, an over-brownness, or a sagging, wilting look. And third, look at the underpart of the stem; it should be free of dirt and discoloration. The whole box should have a nice earthy, fresh smell—as if you had just gone into a deep woods, somewhat dark, somewhat cool, after having taken a walk under a hot sun with no trees to shade you. It is always best to know your greengrocer and to expect from him an honest answer. If he has had the mushrooms for several days—two at the most—you should refuse to buy unless all the enumerated characteristics are present.

Dried mushrooms come into this country in wooden packing boxes or in large bags. In packing boxes they are a delight to the eye. Whether sliced or whole, they are neatly arranged in rows, and the subtlety of their tints and shades gives them an exotic appearance. A whiff, and you are transported into deep woods, to the foot of shadowed boulders, into cool quiet ravines filled with the soft gentle odors of last year's leaves and this year's blossoms. They are so hermetically packed that they retain their shapes a long time. Once removed from their cases, however, they have a tendency to wilt. This is so even of those that are taken out of their large bags and cases and put into small cellophane or wax-paper envelopes for easy retailing. This slight wilting does not in any sense spoil them.

Does the price have anything to do with the quality? As a rule, no. The rarer growths—the cantrelles, the lactarias—will cost more. The price range is very wide, but don't forget that a small quantity goes a long way. As long as they are dry, show no signs of excessive tampering or handling, are fairly clean of dust, and are woody hard, they are worthy of purchase.

Of course, like the fresh growths, the dried ones must not be kept too long. If you have bought more mushrooms than you can use today, put the remainder in a Mason jar, secure the cover, and keep them in a dark, cool place—between 40° and 60°. Theoretically, they would keep forever if not exposed to moisture.

The whole mushrooms come in long strings—the same way garlic or cherry peppers used to be sold. The gatherers immediately run a thread through them and hang them out to dry. The slices are packed only after they have been dried. There are powdered mushrooms, too, but rarely to be had in most shops, being generally sold to hotels and large restaurants.

Canning is a fairly recent process but they may be found in

practically any good food store. They come in three forms: whole, stems only, and coarsely cut pieces of both cap and stem. They are packed in the stock in which they were cooked and the stock itself makes a delicious broth. Cans come in three sizes: 8-ounce, 6-ounce, and 2-ounce. Whole mushrooms are not usually packed in the smaller sizes of cans. The cost compares favorably with that of fresh mushrooms and is much lower than dried ones, although it must be remembered that dried wild mushrooms go a long way. The canned ones are either our American *Agaricus campestris* or the French champignon.

The most recent development has been the advent of freshly frozen mushrooms which are increasingly available in frozen food departments or supermarkets, as well as in the better food shops. The texture is about halfway between that of fresh and canned ones, with the added value of their fresh woodsy flavor being retained. In cooking, slightly less time is needed than for fresh mushrooms. They release a good deal of liquid during thawing; thus, in dishes in which liquid should be kept to a minimum, they should be pre-thawed and patted dry before use. Ideal for soups and stews, where a bit of extra liquid does not matter, they may be added unthawed.

Pickled mushrooms, sold in jars, make splendid hors d'oeuvres. Most of the pickled mushrooms in our shops come from Italy and France or from American growers, the medium being oil or oil and vinegar and, rarely, salt. The Russians pack them in salt in wooden casks immediately after picking and make a great to-do over them with drinks. Serve pickled mushrooms as they come out of the can or with a dash of lemon juice or cayenne pepper.

A word about mushroom sizes: Dried mushrooms come in mixed sizes: button, small, medium, large, all mixed together. Canned mushrooms as well as pickled ones are likely to be only button size, about as large as a small thimble. Fresh ones are graded and put in boxes as: button, small, medium, and large. The recipes in this book will suggest the sizes to employ, so that there is no need to make a statement here. Let it be enough to say that size and taste have nothing to do with each other. For that matter, neither the texture nor the aroma are affected by the fact that you may be eating a pigmy or a giant mushroom.

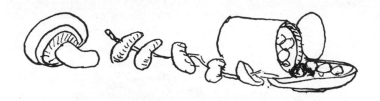

How Expensive Are Mushrooms?

NOT TOO! In season they cost no more than a head of broccoli or of cauliflower. As a matter of fact, they cost no more than 2 or 3 cups of peas, fresh or frozen. Out of season, they occasionally go to fancier prices; but never do they rise to prices beyond the demands of a moderate budget.

Dried mushrooms, of course, are much more expensive by the pound than fresh mushrooms—and a look at the price tag of the imported dried mushrooms may frighten you off. However, when you realize that you buy (and use) so much smaller quantity of the dried than the fresh you can readily compute that there is no great difference in price. The same goes for the canned mushrooms for, like the dried mushrooms, they will go so much farther than the weight on the can would indicate that they are not uncomfortably priced.

Many of the recipes here call for fresh mushrooms, some for dried mushrooms, and some for canned. Ordinarily the three may be interchanged. For your convenience:

3 ounces of any dried
　　　　　mushrooms = 15 ounces of fresh mushrooms
6 to 8 ounces of canned
　mushrooms, whole, in
　　　stems, or in pieces = 1 pound of fresh mushrooms

Fresh mushrooms should sauté or boil gently for 10 minutes *at the very most;* dry mushrooms, after the proper soaking, should sauté or boil 20 minutes; canned mushrooms, since they are already precooked, can sauté or boil only 5 minutes.

Preparing Mushrooms

DO YOU peel fresh mushrooms? Do you cut off any portion? Do you wash them? How do you wash them? Do you dry them before using? If so, how? All these are good questions.

Fresh mushrooms should never be peeled. In that peel is much of the fine flavor. Only the very bottom of the stem need be cut off, and then only if it has turned a bit too brown. If the bottom is tender and clean—cultivated ones invariably are—even the stem need not be touched.

The simplest way of cleaning large mushrooms is to wipe them with damp paper toweling. Wipe them gently, however, since over-brisk or energetic handling will bruise them and cause them to brown quickly. Only if they seem excessively dirty should they be actually washed. To do this, put them in a colander and let a light stream of cold water run over them for a minute or two. Swish them about so that each of them is exposed to the running water and then gently pat them dry between two soft cloths. Never soak fresh mushrooms for any length of time in water. It merely hastens their deterioration.

It is always best to use mushrooms as soon as possible. If they are allowed to stand they turn brown too quickly and, although discoloration does not spoil them, you naturally want them fresh and clean looking.

It is also possible to store them in the refrigerator and keep them quite fresh for several days. Place them on a shallow tray or rack and cover them with dampened paper toweling. Moisten the toweling once every day. It is best not to place them at the very bottom of the refrigerator—it is too cold there—or against anything. A center shelf is ideal, where cold air can pass freely around them. Mushrooms may also be placed in waxed paper cups and kept in the refrigerator for a few days.

Fresh mushrooms may also be frozen and will keep perfectly well for a month or a little longer, but if kept frozen longer they may tend to become rubbery. Mushrooms for freezing should be very firm, white, and fresh. They should not be cleaned or prepared in any way—simply freeze them in their tightly sealed containers.

Another method is best employed for fairly large mushrooms, especially when you are putting them whole on the spits or using them to hold fillings. In either case, take a damp cloth and clean off the separate caps and stems, slicing what you need to slice off—all gently—and then going about your business of using them. An overdamp cloth will cause quick browning; an overbrisk and energetic handling will cause quick bruising. You want neither to happen.

Above all: use your mushrooms as soon as possible after buying them. Do not leave them exposed to the sun or to the

air. Put them, tightly shut in their container, in your refrigerator—where the temperature is no higher than 60° and no lower than 40°—until you plan to ready them for your dish. Under no condition let them stand around after they have been washed. Use them as soon as you can.

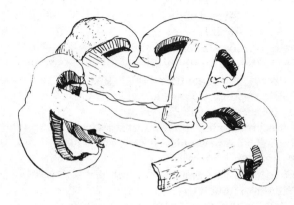

It is particularly important not to peel mushrooms that you intend to broil on spits. The same goes for those you wish to stuff. Removing the skin weakens the structure of the mushrooms, and they will fall apart when you pierce them with the spit or will not hold their shapes when you bake them. The only time you need peel a mushroom is when you intend to serve it raw in a salad.

Slicing mushrooms should be done only in one way. It is best to slice with the knife blade parallel to the stem and running through it. In this way you get larger slices and can get them as thin as wafers. Slicing them across renders the stems almost unusable, since the stem slices will be much smaller than those derived from the caps.

Mushroom stems should never be thrown away, even when the recipe does not call for them. They can be pickled, for one thing, and so served; they can be used in sauces; they make excellent ingredients for stuffings; they are readily adapted to soups. Many recipes here call for stems only.

ALL COOK BOOKS since the beginning of printing have included one or two recipes for mushrooms. All have paid them a courtesy, as it were. But practically no cook book in existence has made a special fuss over them or indicated more than a dozen ways of preparing and eating them.

One reason for this is, of course, the question as to what to call the mushroom—a food item by itself, such as meat or eggs, or a vegetable? Naturally it does belong to the large family of plants except that it contains no chlorophyll. It seems, therefore, to be neither yellow nor green nor red and, in consequence, to present none of the outer semblances of the vegetables used in our cuisine. That it does impart sometimes a penetrating, at other times a pronounced odor goes without saying.

That it has a pleasing texture and a pleasing taste, besides being able to retain agreeable shapes when cut or used whole, also goes without saying. The French make whole meals out of mushrooms, and so do the Italians. The Germans, too, have their steinpilzes and ther pfifferlinges! But to Americans, mushrooms have never seemed to be a whole meal. And it is about time that today, when there are such fine cultivated mushrooms offered, we should decide to find as many uses for them as we can—with zest and gusto.

I have tried to make a collection of recipes that are easy to follow, that offer very little trouble, that are altogether practical and at the same time are most presentable, and that, I trust, are even exciting.

All these recipes have been a part of my personal life; I have tested them all, worked out the quantities of the ingredients to my satisfaction, and served them time and again. Sometimes the recipes are modifications of old ones; most are known the world over. They range from the snack, the hors d'oeuvres, to the soup, the side dish, the combination plate, the whole main course. They are taste-appealing, eye-appealing, and they go easy on the digestion—altogether a satisfying addition to your repertoire. Here's hoping!

❀ Broiled Mushroom Hors d'Oeuvres

TO SERVE 6

6 large mushrooms
1/4 cup of well-seasoned stock
Salt
Touch of cayenne pepper
2 tablespoons of butter
1/4 cup of bread crumbs
6 toast rounds

Remove mushroom stems and carefully scoop out mushroom insides. Mince together and, in a small saucepan, boil with seasonings in stock for 5 minutes. While this boils, sauté mushroom caps in a frying pan slowly in 1 tablespoon of butter for 5 minutes. Drain stems, pouring stock into a small, shallow baking pan. In this, place mushroom caps, top side down. Fill them with cooked stems, cover with bread crumbs, and dot with remaining butter. Broil 3 minutes, 3 inches below a high flame. Serve very hot on toast rounds.

Variations

(1) With the minced stems, mix 1 tablespoon of minced parsley, 1/2 teaspoon of grated lemon rind, and 1 tablespoon of minced pimiento. Proceed as above.

(2) Combine 1/4 cup of bread crumbs with butter, stock, minced stems, salt, and cayenne, and sauté over a low flame. Proceed as above, filling caps with this mixture and topping with a sprinkling of minced pimiento.

(3) Sauté mushroom caps as above. Lay them in stock in a shallow pan. Combine minced stems, bread crumbs, and seasonings, pour over caps, and dot with butter. Brown under broiler flame for 2 minutes.

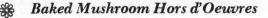

❋ Baked Mushroom Hors d'Oeuvres

Served cold, this is a pleasant addition to an antipasto. Served hot, this makes a main dish for 2 persons.

TO SERVE 8

8 large mushrooms
6 green olives, minced
1 can of anchovy fillets
6 tablespoons of bread crumbs
6 tablespoons of olive oil or 3 of butter

Remove mushroom stems and carefully scoop out insides of mushrooms. Mince together with anchovy fillets and mix with olives, bread crumbs, and a small amount of oil. With this mixture, fill mushroom caps. Place caps in a baking dish, filled side up. Pour remaining oil over mushrooms, making sure some spills over into baking dish. Bake in a 350° oven for 20 minutes. If tops are not brown, place under broiler flame for 1 minute. Serve hot on individual plates.

❀ *Creamed Mushroom Hors d'Oeuvres, Piquante*

TO SERVE 6

1 teaspoon of flour
1/2 cup of well-seasoned stock—at room temperature
1/2 cup of heavy cream—at room temperature
1 cup of mushroom stems, minced
12 green olives, minced
Salt
Touch of cayenne pepper
6 slices of toast, crusts trimmed off
Sprinkle of paprika

In the top of a double boiler, directly over the flame, blend flour, stock, and cream. Assemble double boiler and heat gradually until mixture thickens smoothly. Add mushrooms and cook, covered, for 10 minutes. Uncover and stir well to make sure mixture is still smooth. Allow 5 to 10 minutes for it to thicken again. Then add minced olives, salt, and cayenne. Serve on toast with a sprinkle of paprika.

Creamed Mushroom Hors d'Oeuvres with Wine

TO SERVE 4

1 1/2 tablespoons of flour
1 tablespoon of butter
1 cup of light cream or whole milk, scalded
2 cups of mushroom stems, minced
Salt
1/8 teaspoon of powdered nutmeg
1/4 cup of dry sherry
4 slices of toast

In the top of a double boiler, directly over the flame, blend flour and butter carefully. Assemble double boiler and gradually add scalded cream. Before mixture thickens, add mushrooms and seasonings. Cook, uncovered, until fairly thick. Add sherry, stir vigorously, and serve on toast.

❀ *Deep-fried Mushroom Hors d'Oeuvres*

This adds zest to any antipasto, but it can also be a main dish. In that case, prepare and serve 4 large mushrooms to a person (increasing all ingredients proportionately) and serve on buttered toast or noodles.

TO SERVE 4

12 small mushrooms
Salt and pepper
1/4 cup of well-seasoned stock
1/4 cup of fine bread crumbs
1 egg, well beaten
Fat for deep frying
Sprinkle of nutmeg
12 small toast rounds

Salt and pepper the mushrooms. Place in stock in a small saucepan and boil gently for 5 minutes. Drain well. Dip mushrooms in bread crumbs, then in egg, and again in crumbs. Set aside. Heat fat to a high heat in an appropriate deep pan. Drop in mushrooms and fry until golden brown. Drain on brown paper, sprinkle with nutmeg, and serve on toast rounds.

❀ Deviled Mushrooms

This may be served as an hors d'oeuvre or as a condiment with meat or fish. The proportions given will make 4 generous servings or 6 small ones.

> *1 pound of small mushrooms, whole*
> *1 cup of meat stock*
> *1 tablespoon of flour*
> *2 teaspoons of dry mustard*
> *1/2 cup of skim milk*
> *2 tablespoons of white-wine vinegar or white vinegar*
> *2 tablespoons of olive oil*
> *1/8 teaspoon of cayenne pepper*

In a covered saucepan, boil mushrooms in stock for 10 minutes. Meanwhile, in a cup or bowl, combine all other ingredients in order, beginning with flour blended with mustard, adding each slowly and stirring constantly to keep smooth. Drain mushrooms thoroughly and add to mixture. Refrigerate.

Note

You may heat the milk and flour over the fire, cool, and then add mustard. Proceed as above.

❀ *Glazed Spiced Mushrooms*

This is a condiment—to be served with a fatty meat, such as ham or duck.

TO SERVE 6

2 tablespoons of butter
1 teaspoon of flour
1/8 teaspoon of powdered nutmeg
1/8 teaspoon of powdered ginger
1 tablespoon of brown sugar
1 1/2 pounds of small mushrooms, whole
1/4 cup of dry sherry

In a skillet over a low flame, soften butter and blend in flour. Add spices, sugar, and (keeping flame low) mushrooms. Turn carefully so each takes on color. At the end of 10 minutes, add sherry, mix well, and serve.

✿ Pickled Mushrooms

Pickled mushrooms can be served cold the day you make them or kept almost indefinitely under refrigeration. They can be served as part of an antipasto tray (with toothpicks, if eaten with cocktails), or they can be served as a condiment with fish or bland meat.

TO MAKE 2 PINTS

3 pounds of mushrooms—the button variety is best. (If larger ones are used, cut off ends of stems.)

White vinegar
Olive oil
1 tablespoon of mixed pickling spice

Put mushrooms in saucepan and cover with a mixture of half vinegar and half hot water. Salt to taste. Boil 15 minutes. Drain liquid off into another pan. Cool mushrooms.

Meanwhile, put a small wooden spoon to soak in the liquid to sterilize it. Mix together equal parts of olive oil and vinegar (less than 2 cups should do) and add spice. Fill sterilized jar one quarter full with liquid. Add mushrooms, packing them down with the small wooden spoon that has been soaking. (With a wooden spoon, mushrooms will neither break nor lose their shape.) Fill jar to overflowing with remainder of oil-vinegar mixture. Cover and store in a cool place.

✿ *Mushroom Relish*

This will keep for several weeks under refrigeration and can be served with any dry meat or fish requiring added zest.

TO MAKE 2 PINTS

2 1/2 cups of pickled mushrooms (see preceding page)
1/2 cup of minced raw peppers, green or red
1/2 cup of minced green olives
1/2 cup of minced black olives
1/2 teaspoon of powdered nutmeg
1/2 teaspoon of powdered mace
1/8 teaspoon of powdered ginger
1/8 teaspoon of freshly ground black pepper
1 small sweet gherkin, minced fine
1 small pickled onion, minced fine
2 tablespoons of dry sauterne or French vermouth

Combine all ingredients and fill jar, making sure both it and the cover are sterilized.

❀ *Raw Mushroom Salad*

You will be pleasantly surprised if this is your introduction to a mushroom salad.

TO SERVE 4

1 pound of mushrooms—caps only. (Reserve stems for future use.) *

1/4 cup of vinegar—preferably white-wine vinegar

1/2 cup of olive oil

Dash of cayenne pepper

Salt and pepper

Lettuce leaves

1 tablespoon of minced pimiento

1 tablespoon of pickled capers or of nasturium seeds (washed and drained)

2 hard-boiled eggs

Peel mushroom caps and slice thin. Marinate slices in vinegar, oil, and seasonings (the marinade should be covered) for 1 hour in refrigerator. At the same time, chill lettuce leaves. Arrange lettuce in a bowl and mound mushrooms in the center. Pour over marinade. Decorate with pimiento and capers. Quarter eggs lengthwise and ring them around mushrooms. Serve cold.

* Recipes which call for mushroom stems only are on pages 22, 23, 32, 39, 40, 41, 80, 81, 88, 94, 105, 112, 119, and 120.

❋ *Pickled Mushroom Salad*

TO SERVE 6

> *Crisp lettuce leaves*
> *2 cups of pickled mushrooms (see page 27)*
> *1 cup of pimientos, sliced*
> *1 tablespoon of pickled capers, washed*
> *1/3 cup of salad dressing, French or Italian (see below)*
> *12 toast sticks*

On a flat platter arrange lettuce leaves. Mound pimientos in the center and ring with mushrooms. Decorate with capers. Pour dressing over all and then make an outer ring around the platter of the toast sticks.

> *Italian Dressing*
> *6 tablespoons of olive oil*
> *2 tablespoons of red or white vinegar, or of lemon juice*
> *Salt and pepper*
> *1 clove of garlic*
> *Pinch of oregano, basil, bay leaf, finnocchio seeds, or
>   celery seeds only if desired*
> *Screw-cap jar*

In the jar, mix oil and vinegar, adding salt and pepper to taste. Add garlic, whole, and herbs. Shake well before using. Store in refrigerator.

Mushrooms with Salsa Verde

TO SERVE 4

16 large mushrooms
1 large onion
Salt and pepper
Lettuce leaves
1 cup of Salsa Verde (below)

Remove mushroom stems and chop them with the onion very fine. Barely cover with water. Salt and pepper to taste. In a large skillet, place mushroom caps. Over them pour onion, stems, and water, and stew for 15 minutes, covered. Chill. Serve on lettuce leaves and cover with Salsa Verde.

Salsa Verde

1/4 bunch of crisp watercress
1/2 cup of crisp parsley—leaves only
1 clove of garlic
3 tablespoons of olive oil
1 tablespoon of lemon juice

In a wooden bowl chop greens and garlic until almost a liquid. Add olive oil, drop by drop, stirring well. Add lemon juice and spoon over mushrooms.

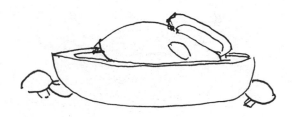

✿ Clear Mushroom Bouillon

This bouillon can be served hot with a topping of julienned chicken, or it can be used as the base for a creamed mushroom soup or for gravy.

TO SERVE 6

4 cups of mushroom stems (1 pound or more), coarsely minced
1 breast of chicken with wings, all skin removed
2 tablespoons of chopped parsley
1 small onion, minced coarsely
Salt
6 cups of boiling water

Put all ingredients in a deep saucepan and cover tightly. Bring to a boil, reduce flame, and simmer for 1 hour. Remove chicken and strain liquid twice through an extremely fine sieve. Run mushrooms, parsley, and onion through the finest knives of your grinder, collecting the liquid. Strain this three times through triple-mesh cheesecloth. Combine with first liquid. Heat 5 minutes and serve. If you wish, julienne the chicken and add to bouillon.

❀ Cream of Mushroom Soup

TO SERVE 6

1 level tablespoon of butter
1 small onion, minced almost to a liquid
1 level tablespoon of flour
1/8 teaspoon of powdered nutmeg
Salt
4 cups of milk, scalded
1/2 pound of mushrooms, sliced thin and then minced
1 cup of heavy cream
Bread sticks or croutons

In the top of a double boiler, directly over the flame, melt butter and add onion. Slowly add flour, nutmeg, and salt. Gradually add scalded milk, stirring to keep mixture smooth. Assemble double boiler, add mushrooms, cover, and cook for 15 minutes. Pour in cream and stir until well heated. Serve with bread sticks or croutons.

Variations

(1) *Soup Supreme:* Add 1/8 teaspoon of ginger to butter, flour, and seasoning, omitting the onion. Use 4 cups of mushroom bouillon (page 32) instead of milk. At the end, add 1/4 cup of cognac and sprinkle each serving with julienned olives.

(2) For a lighter soup, substitute for the 1 cup of heavy cream 1/2 cup of milk and 1/2 cup of heavy cream, or a 5th cup of milk. Sprinkle with nutmeg.

(3) *Romanian:* Substitute 2 cups of tomato juice for 2 cups of milk. Cook all ingredients together in a double boiler or saucepan for 20 minutes. In each soup bowl, float a slice of toast topped with 1 tablespoon of sour cream sprinkled with paprika.

❀ Spiced Cream of Mushroom Soup

Serve very hot or very cold.

TO SERVE 6

3 cups of milk—at room temperature
2 cups of well-seasoned chicken stock—at room temper-
ature
1/2 pound of mushrooms, cut up coarsely
Bouquet garni of coriander, bay leaves, several whole
cloves, bits of nutmeg, tied in a small cheesecloth bag
1 heaping tablespoon of butter
1 tablespoon of flour
1/8 teaspoon of pepper
Salt

In a double boiler, mix milk and stock, scald, and set aside. In
a saucepan, cook mushrooms with bouquet garni in boiling
water to cover for 5 minutes. Remove cheesecloth bag, dis-
carding its contents. Combine milk, stock, and mushrooms and
cook for 10 minutes slowly. In a large saucepan, blend butter
and flour over a low flame, carefully stirring in some of the
liquid. When smooth, slowly pour in remaining liquid, stirring constantly to avoid lumping. Simmer for about 20 minutes
more. Season to taste.

✿ *Mushroom Vichysoisse*

Whether you serve this hot or cold, it is delicious.

TO SERVE 4

1 level tablespoon of butter
3 tablespoons of finely minced onion, or of leeks or chives
1 cup of seasoned mashed potatoes
1 cup of milk, scalded
1/2 pound of mushrooms, minced fine
1 cup of rich stock
1/2 cup of light cream
1 tablespoon of minced parsley

Work butter and onion into mashed potatoes. Slowly add scalded milk. Cook in a double boiler for 5 minutes. Meanwhile, in a saucepan, boil mushrooms in stock for 10 minutes. Add them to milk and potatoes and heat thoroughly. Add cream, garnish with parsley, and serve.

✿ *Mushroom and Barley Soup*

TO SERVE 6

1/2 cup of barley
2 quarts of well-seasoned stock, strained of all fat
1/2 pound of mushrooms, cut up coarsely
1 tablespoon of shredded carrots
1 tablespoon of minced celery
1 tablespoon of shredded parsley
1/8 teaspoon of powdered nutmeg
Salt
Croutons

Carefully wash barley in a sieve under running water. Cook it in 1 1/2 quarts of stock—covered and slowly—for 1 1/4 to 1 1/2 hours. In remaining stock, cook mushrooms, carrots, celery, and parsley—covered and very fast—for 15 minutes. Mix this with barley and season with nutmeg. Salt, bring to a boil, and serve topped with croutons.

Variations
(1) To this recipe, add 1/2 cup of cooked peas, or cooked string beans, or cooked celery, each with some of the juice in which it has been cooked.

(2) For the barley, substitute 1/2 cup of raw rice, or raw wheat germ, or buckwheat groats (Kasha).

(3) Make up 1/2 cup of barley and wheat germ or of barley and groats and substitute for the barley alone.

(4) If you have leftover chicken, beef, or veal, cut into bean-size pieces or julienne, and add long enough before the end to heat thoroughly.

Mushroom and Fish Chowder

TO SERVE 6

1 tablespoon of olive oil
1/2 clove of garlic, crushed almost to a pulp
1/2 cup of onions, sliced very thin
1 small green pepper, diced
2 ribs of celery, diced
1/2 cup of fresh peas
Salt and pepper
1 pound of very small whole mushrooms
2 pounds of firm fish—haddock, shad, sea bass, carp, or the tail of a halibut—cut into small chunks and thoroughly dried
1/2 cup of whole or skim milk
1 cup of fish stock or clear bouillon
1/4 teaspoon of powdered ginger
1 ounce of brandy or cognac (optional)

In a broad, low saucepan, heat oil and in it sauté garlic, onions, green pepper, celery, and peas for 10 minutes, covered, over a low flame. Salt and pepper lightly, add mushrooms, and cook 10 minutes longer, still covered. Now add the pieces of fish, salt and pepper them, cover, and cook another 10 minutes. Uncover and cook 5 minutes at slightly higher heat. In another saucepan, bring milk and stock to a boil. Pour over the fish. Mix ginger with brandy, shut off flame, pour this into the chowder, and serve in soup plates.

Variation

Some people may wish to increase the amount of ginger and to thicken the chowder. Double the quantity of ginger and add 1 tablespoon of flour or cornstarch, blending this in a cup, off the fire, with some of the stock.

✿ Mushroom and Oyster Stew

TO SERVE 6

1 pound of small whole mushrooms
2 tablespoons of butter
1/2 teaspoon of salt
1/8 teaspoon of pepper
2 dozen plump raw oysters, shelled and carefully dried
1 cup of milk, scalded
1 cup of clear bouillon, heated to a boil
1 ounce of brandy (optional)

In a skillet, melt butter and add mushrooms, salt, and pepper. Cover and cook briskly over rather high heat, tossing several times. After 10 minutes, uncover, add oysters, and toss well again. Cover and cook 3 minutes. Add scalded milk and stock, bring to a quick boil, uncovered. Add brandy if used and serve immediately.

❀ Mushroom Sauce I

This and the two sauces that follow are good with any broiled meat and especially with steak. Of course, mushroom stems can be substituted in all five sauce recipes.

TO MAKE 1 CUP

1/4 pound of mushrooms, sliced wafer thin
1/2 cup of seasoned stock
Salt and pepper
1 tablespoon of butter
1/4 teaspoon of flour

In a skillet, cook mushrooms and stock over very low flame for 10 minutes. In a cup, cream butter, seasonings, and flour. Slowly blend in some of the mushroom stock until mixture is smooth and thin. Pour into mushrooms, stirring constantly and keeping flame low. When piping hot, pour over steak.

❀ Mushroom Sauce II

TO MAKE 1 CUP

1 tablespoon of butter
1 small onion, sliced very thin in the round
1/4 clove of garlic, mashed
1/4 pound of mushrooms, sliced wafer thin
1/2 cup of seasoned stock
Pinch of nutmeg
Salt and pepper

In a skillet, melt butter and in this soften onion and garlic. Add mushrooms, raising flame slightly, and sauté 15 minutes or until they begin to color. Slowly add stock, stirring gently. Season, bring to a fast boil, and turn off flame. Pour over steak or serve in a gravy boat.

39

❄ *Mushroom Sauce with Wine I*

Substitute mushroom stems on this and next two recipes if they are at hand.

TO MAKE 1 CUP

1 tablespoon of butter
1 onion, sliced thin in the round
1/4 pound of mushrooms, sliced wafer thin
1/3 cup of sherry
1/8 teaspoon of nutmeg
1/8 teaspoon of mace
Salt

In a skillet, melt butter and in it brown onion. Do not burn. Add mushrooms and sauté gently for 15 minutes. Now, gradually thin out with sherry, season, and pour over meat.

❄ *Mushroom Sauce with Wine II*

This sauce is delicious with beef roast, and good with any roast, since it uses the natural gravy from the roasting pan.

TO MAKE 3 CUPS

2 tablespoons of butter
1 onion, minced almost to a liquid
1/2 pound of mushrooms, sliced wafer thin
2 cups of natural gravy from the roast
Salt and pepper
2 ounces of dry red wine—preferably claret

In a frying pan, melt butter and stir in onion. Add mushrooms and sauté gently for 15 minutes or more until mushrooms have yielded some of their liquid. Add gravy, season, and bring to a boil. Stir in the wine and serve in a gravy boat.

❁ *Mushroom Sauce with Wine III*

This is especially good with chicken or a roast.

TO MAKE 2 CUPS

1 tablespoon of butter
1 tablespoon of minced parsley
1/2 clove of garlic, minced
1 small onion, minced
1 heaping teaspoon of flour
1 cup of clear, rich stock
1/8 teaspoon of powdered nutmeg
1/4 pound of mushrooms, sliced wafer thin
1/4 cup of marsala, sauterne, or sherry
Salt

In a skillet, melt butter. Mix minced parsley, garlic, and onion well and sauté in butter briefly over a medium flame. Blend flour with a small amount of stock until it is smooth and thin. Pour into butter mixture, stirring vigorously. Gradually add remaining stock, stirring constantly to keep sauce smooth. Add mushrooms and lower flame. Season with salt and nutmeg. Cook for 10 minutes, add wine, bring to a boil, and serve in a gravy boat.

Note

In this sauce, truffles may be substituted for mushrooms. Use 1/2 ounce only.

❋ Mushroom and Oil Sauce

What you have here will be sufficient to pour over 1 1/2 pounds of spaghetti or other pasta and will serve 6 people. Grated cheese makes a good topping, both for this and the following recipe.

TO SERVE 6

1 cup of olive oil or of melted butter
1 pound of mushrooms, minced
3 cloves of garlic, minced
Salt and pepper

In a deep saucepan, heat oil slowly. Then add mushrooms and garlic, and brown for 5 minutes. Season. Lower flame and simmer for 10 minutes. Sauce is now ready for the pasta.

❀ *Mushroom and Tomato Sauce*

This sauce, which goes with any pasta, requires 1 1/2 hours of cooking time.

TO SERVE 6

2 tablespoons of olive oil
2 onions, sliced in the round
2 cloves of garlic, whole
1 pound of button mushrooms, whole, or of larger mushrooms, sliced
1 #3 can (4 cups) of tomatoes
1 #2 can (2 1/2 cups) of tomato juice
1/2 can of tomato paste and an equal amount of water
Salt and pepper

In a deep saucepan, bring olive oil to a high heat. In it, soften onions and garlic, making sure not to brown. Add mushrooms, cover, and cook for 15 minutes—very slowly. Stir occasionally. Remove cover, salt slightly, and boil rapidly for 5 minutes at a high heat, stirring frequently. Add tomatoes and simmer for 15 minutes. Pour in tomato juice and simmer for 15 more minutes. Add tomato paste and water and simmer for another 30 minutes. Salt and pepper to taste.

Note

Except for the 5-minute period of rapid boiling to permit evaporation of some of the mushroom liquid, the cooking should be *slow.*

❋ *Mushroom and Seafood Sauce*

This makes a very tasty dish when served over boiled rice or spaghetti.

TO SERVE 6

2 cloves of garlic
4 tablespoons of olive oil, butter, or margarine
1 large onion, sliced in the round
1 pound of mushrooms, thinly sliced
1 #3 can (4 cups) of hard-packed tomatoes, pulp only
Salt
Cayenne pepper
1 level tablespoon of oregano or thyme
1 pound of shrimp, cut up small or
1/2 pound of crab, lobster, or any flaked fillet of fish

Brown garlic in olive oil and remove. Soften onion in the oil but do not brown. Add tomato pulp and cook slowly for 15 minutes. Add seasonings and after 5 minutes more add the seafood. Cook slowly for another 15 minutes. Add mushrooms and cook gently for 5 minutes.

Mushrooms under Bell

As a rule, this dish calls for wild mushrooms, but the cultivated field mushrooms or champignons do well too.

Mushrooms served under bell look as in the picture below. Serving under bell preserves the full aroma of the mushrooms. If instead of bells you use ramekins, lay a piece of toast on the bottom, fill the ramekins with the mushroom mixture, cover tightly, and so serve.

TO SERVE 4

2 tablespoons of butter
1/2 teaspoon of flour
1/8 teaspoon of powdered nutmeg
1/8 teaspoon of freshly ground pepper
Salt
16 large mushroom caps (Reserve stems for other purposes.) *
1/4 cup of sherry, marsala, or madeira
4 slices of dry toast

Blend butter and flour in a saucepan over a low flame. Add seasonings and then mushrooms, making sure each cap is colored with the butter mixture. Add wine and cover very tightly. (Place a piece of heavy brown paper over the skillet and then press down the cover.) After 15 minutes remove cover, place toast slices on warm plates, cover with mushroom and liquid, and then tightly with the bell.

* Recipes which call for mushroom stems only are on pages 22, 23, 32, 39, 40, 41, 80, 81, 88, 94, 105, 112, 119, and 120.

❀ Sautéed Mushrooms

A universal dish, and the simplest and most often used way of serving mushrooms. There is no reason why it should not be perfect. Serve on toast if a main dish, or serve as a side dish.

TO SERVE 4

1/3 cup of olive oil or 3 tablespoons of melted butter
*1 1/2 pounds of mushrooms—whole, if button variety,
     otherwise, sliced*
Salt

In a skillet, bring oil to a high heat. Drop in mushrooms gently, rolling them in the oil. Cover, reduce flame, and cook slowly for 10 minutes. Uncover and raise flame, stirring frequently until mushrooms become golden in color and liquid evaporates. Season and serve very hot.

Variations

(1) Brown 1 or 2 cloves of crushed garlic in the fat and remove before adding mushrooms.

(2) Slice in a small onion just before the final cooking.

TO SERVE 6

*1 1/2 pounds of large mushrooms, sliced very thin, or of
    button mushrooms, whole*
3 tablespoons of olive oil or butter
Salt and pepper
*1 tablespoon of tomato paste, melted in 2 tablespoons of
    stock or boiling water*
3 tablespoons of grated cheese, preferably parmesan
6 slices of toast

In a large skillet, slowly sauté mushrooms in oil or butter with seasoning for 15 minutes, uncovered. Add tomato paste mixture and cook slowly for 5 minutes. Add the cheese and cook, still slowly, for 10 minutes. Serve on toast.

Variation

Those who enjoy the flavor of a liqueur with their mushrooms will wish to omit the tomato paste and add a dash of cognac. Sauté mushrooms as directed above. Add the cheese and cook for 5 minutes, stirring constantly. Add the cognac and then serve over plain buttered rice or noodles.

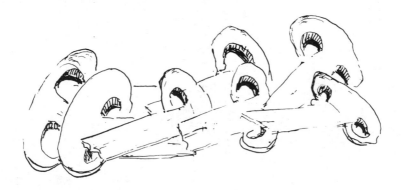

✾ Sautéed Mushrooms with Sour Cream

This is a Russian variation of a world-popular recipe.

TO SERVE 6

1 1/2 pounds of small mushrooms, whole
1/2 cup of sweet butter
1 tablespoon of white-wine vinegar
1/8 teaspoon of cayenne pepper
1/8 teaspoon of powdered ginger
Salt
1 cup of sour cream
1 teaspoon of paprika

In a skillet, sauté mushrooms in butter over a moderate flame. When mushrooms have absorbed some of the butter, cover and cook slowly for 10 minutes. Uncover, add all seasonings except paprika, and simmer 10 minutes more. Remove from fire and pour onto a hot platter. Cover with sour cream and sprinkle with paprika.

❀ *Sautéed Mushrooms with Hard-boiled Eggs*

TO SERVE 6

3 tablespoons of olive oil or melted butter
1 small onion, minced to a pulp
1 1/2 pounds of button mushrooms
Salt
Dash of cayenne pepper
3 hard-boiled eggs, chopped coarse
6 slices of buttered toast

In a skillet, slowly heat olive oil and onion. In this, sauté mushrooms until a golden brown—about 15 minutes over a moderate flame. At this point, season and add eggs. Reduce flame and when eggs are heated serve on toast.

❀ *Mushrooms Sautéed with Ground Meat*

This is a simple dish, but incomparable in flavor and texture. You need not hesitate to serve it to guests, preferably over rice or noodles or toast.

TO SERVE 4

Piece of beef suet, or 3 ounces of diced pork lard, or 2 tablespoons of butter
3/4 pound of any ground meat, rather lean
Salt and pepper
1 pound of mushrooms, minced
1 tablespoon of parsley

In a skillet, render suet or lard. Season meat and sauté in fat until brown. Add mushrooms and parsley. Sauté 15 minutes longer and serve.

❀ Sautéed Mushrooms with Mint

This in another mushroom dish that does excellently when served over plain buttered rice or noodles.

TO SERVE 4

1 teaspoon of chervil, minced to a liquid
1 teaspoon of mint leaves, minced to a liquid
1 tablespoon of sweet *butter*
1 1/2 pounds of large mushrooms, sliced wafer thin
1/2 cup of chicken stock
Touch of powdered nutmeg
Salt and pepper

Work chervil and mint into butter and melt in a skillet over a low flame. Add mushrooms and sauté gently for 15 minutes. Add stock and seasonings, bring to a boil, and serve.

❀ Sautéed Mushrooms with Wine

TO SERVE 4

3 tablespoons of butter
1 teaspoon of flour
1 1/2 pounds of mushrooms, whole
Salt
1/4 cup of sherry, madeira, or marsala wine
1/8 teaspoon of powdered nutmeg and clove combined

In a large skillet, melt butter over a low flame and carefully stir in flour. Add mushrooms, one at a time, turning each over to absorb some of the butter. Cover with water, salt, and cover skillet tightly. Cook slowly for 10 minutes. Uncover, increase flame, and cook until liquid has been appreciably reduced. Add wine and spice, bring to a vigorous boil, and serve immediately so as to preserve both the aroma and the heat.

✾ *Sautéed Mushrooms with Chestnuts and Wine*

TO SERVE 4

2 tablespoons of butter
1 pound of button mushrooms
18 fresh chestnuts—parboiled, skinned, and boiled 45
    minutes, or until tender
Salt
1/4 cup of very dry sherry or of dry white wine

In a skillet, melt butter over a low flame. In this, heat mushrooms until they take on color, cook slowly for about 10
minutes. Uncover, add drained chestnuts, and very little salt.
Toss 2 or 3 times. When chestnuts are heated through, add
sherry, bring to a brisk boil, and serve.

Variation

If you prefer to use dried chestnuts, this recipe will do better.
Soak chestnuts (1/2 pound) for 1 hour in warm water.
Change water and boil 30 minutes or until tender. Drain
thoroughly. For the butter, substitute 1 tablespoon of minced
ham or bacon. Render this slowly and proceed as above. After
adding chestnuts, season with 1/8 teaspoon of nutmeg. Add
wine immediately and cook slowly for 10 minutes.

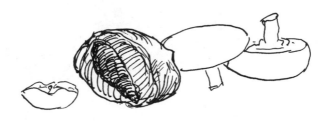

This can be served over plain boiled rice, spaghetti, noodles, or toast.

TO SERVE 4

3 tablespoons of olive oil or melted butter
1 onion, minced fine
1 pound of small mushrooms, whole, or of large ones, quartered
1/2 pound of unsalted nuts—almonds, Brazil, filberts, or pignole
Salt and pepper
Pinch of nutmeg

In a skillet, melt butter and add onion. Do not brown. Add mushrooms and sauté over fairly high flame, uncovered, for 15 minutes until golden color. (Mushrooms need watching and stirring to avoid burning.) Add nuts and seasonings and heat thoroughly.

❀ Broiled Mushrooms

After sautéing, broiling is, probably, the second most universal way of preparing mushrooms. Those who season them properly have a very tasty dish.

TO SERVE 4

1 1/2 pounds of large mushrooms (the larger the better)
—caps only. (Reserve stems for other uses.) *
3 tablespoons of olive oil or melted butter
Salt and pepper
4 slices of toast

Lay the mushroom caps on the grid of your broiler pan, brush with oil, and season with salt and pepper. Broil at a high heat, 3 inches below the flame, for 4 minutes on each side. Serve piping hot on buttered toast.

* Recipes which call for mushroom stems only are on pages 22, 23, 32, 39, 40, 41, 80, 81, 88, 94, 105, 112, 119, and 120.

❀ *Broiled Mushrooms and Onions*

TO SERVE 4

1 1/2 pounds of large mushrooms
8 thin slices of Bermuda onion
1/2 cup of bread crumbs
1 clove of garlic, minced fine
4 tablespoons of clear stock
1/2 cup of olive oil or of melted butter
Salt and pepper

Slice mushrooms from top to bottom so that the stems remain part of the slices. In a shallow baking dish, spread onion slices. Mix together bread crumbs and garlic and sprinkle over onions. Over this pour stock and then 1/4 cup of oil. Lay on mushrooms and over them pour remaining oil. Season. Place in broiler, 3 inches below the flame, and broil 8 minutes.

❊ *Broiled Mushrooms Stuffed with Fish*

TO SERVE 4

16 large mushroom caps. (Reserve stems for other uses.) *
3 tablespoons of butter
1/2 pound of leftover boiled fresh cod, haddock, or
*   flounder fillets, flaked small*
1 teaspoon of sweet marjoram
1 cup of fine bread crumbs
1 tablespoon of dried currants, steeped in warm water for
*   10 minutes and drained dry*
Salt and pepper
Toast sticks

In a skillet, sauté the mushroom caps for 10 minutes in 2 tablespoons of butter. Meanwhile, combine all other ingredients,
except toast sticks. Fill mushroom caps with this mixture. Place
in a shallow buttered baking pan and dot with remaining butter. Broil mushrooms for 3 minutes. Serve with toast sticks.

    * Recipes which call for mushroom stems only are on pages 22, 23, 32,
39, 40, 41, 80, 81, 88, 94, 105, 112, 119, and 120.

TO SERVE 4

2 ounces of salt pork, cubed
8 quahogs (or 16 Little Neck) clams, minced fine and
    without the juice
1 rib of celery, minced fine
1 small onion, minced fine
1 teaspoon of flour
1/2 cup of heavy cream
16 large mushroom caps. (Reserve stems for other uses.) *
1/2 cup of fine bread crumbs
Cayenne pepper

In a skillet, render pork. Remove crackles and combine them with clams, celery, and onion. In the fat, blend flour and gradually add cream, stirring to keep the mixture smooth. Add the clam mixture. Broil mushroom caps on a grill, tops up, for 2 minutes. Remove from broiler, turn over, and fill caps with clam mixture, covering with bread crumbs seasoned with cayenne. Broil 3 minutes and serve.

* Recipes which call for mushroom stems only are on pages 22, 23, 32, 39, 40, 41, 80, 81, 88, 94, 105, 112, 119, and 120.

This is really just a variation of broiled mushrooms but has an eye appeal which makes it different. Mushrooms cooked this way can be served either on a bed of plain buttered rice or on toast.

TO SERVE 4

*1 1/2 pounds of medium-size mushrooms—caps only. (Reserve stems for other uses.) ***
1/3 cup of olive oil or melted butter
Salt and pepper

You must *not* skin the mushrooms for this dish, because skinning causes them to crack open when placed on a skewer. Use one long skewer per person and string one fourth of the mushrooms on each skewer. Brush with oil and broil. If you have an infrared broiler, fine. If not, lay skewers across a baking pan thus:

Place pan 3 inches below broiler flame and broil for 8 minutes, turning skewers 3 or 4 times.

Variations

(1) Alternate mushrooms with slices of raw red or green peppers (or small whole peppers), brushing these also with the oil.

(2) In addition to (or in place of) the peppers, use halves of small white onions.

* Recipes which call for mushroom stems only are on pages 22, 23, 32, 39, 40, 41, 80, 81, 88, 94, 105, 112, 119, and 120.

❋ Spitted Mushrooms with Vegetables

TO SERVE 6

18 large mushroom caps—do not peel. (Reserve stems for
*sauce.) ***

18 pieces of raw green or sweet red peppers, the diameter
of the caps

9 tomatoes—very hard—sliced in half, the diameter of the
caps

1/2 cup of olive oil or melted butter

1 tablespoon of salt, pepper, and garlic powder (not garlic
salt), combined to taste

Skewer caps, peppers, and tomatoes alternately on spits. See
preceding page if you are using spits over a baking pan. Brush
with oil and sprinkle with mixed seasonings. Broil 3 inches below flame for 8 minutes, turning spits 3 or 4 times. Serve
covered with sauce made of stems according to recipe for Sauce
II on page 39.

* Recipes which call for mushroom stems only are on pages 22, 23, 32,
39, 40, 41, 80, 81, 88, 94, 105, 112, 119, and 120.

Again, in this recipe it is important that the mushrooms be un-peeled.

TO   SERVE   6

18 large mushroom caps. (Reserve stems for sauce.) *
3 pounds of top sirloin, veal, or lamb—without bone or
fat and cut up into pieces about the diameter and
thickness of the mushroom caps
3 tablespoons of melted butter
Salt and pepper

If you have an infrared broiler, you will not need spits. If you do not, see page 57 for arranging spits over a baking pan. Alternate mushroom caps and meat rounds on spits, brush with melted butter, sprinkle generously with salt and pepper, and broil 8 minutes for beef, 12 minutes for veal, and 14 minutes for lamb. During the broiling process, brush occasionally with butter and turn spits 3 or 4 times. Make a sauce with the stems, following the recipe for Sauce II on page 39, and pour over mushrooms and meat while serving.

* Recipes which call for mushroom stems only are on pages 22, 23, 32, 39, 40, 41, 80, 81, 88, 94, 105, 112, 119, and 120.

❀ *Baked Whole Mushrooms*

This can be a satisfying meal by itself, especially if served with buttered rice, spaghetti, or plain noodles.

TO SERVE 4

1 1/2 pounds of small-size mushrooms
2 cups of seasoned chicken stock
Salt and pepper

Dry mushrooms very thoroughly. In a deep casserole, mix mushrooms, stock, and seasonings. Bake in a 350° oven for 20 minutes.

Variation
Sprinkle mushrooms with buttered bread crumbs and dot with pimiento.

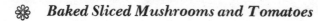
❀ *Baked Sliced Mushrooms and Tomatoes*

TO SERVE 4

6 large tomatoes—peeled or not, as you please
1 clove of garlic, minced
Salt and pepper
1/3 cup of olive oil or melted butter
1 pound of large mushrooms sliced from top to bottom
1/2 cup of bread crumbs
1/2 cup of well-seasoned stock

Slice tomatoes in the round, as thin as possible. Lay them on bottom of a baking pan. Sprinkle with garlic, salt, and pepper. Pour over most of the oil, reserving a small amount for the mushrooms. Top with sliced mushrooms and cover with bread crumbs. Moisten with stock and remaining oil. Bake in a 350° oven for 15 minutes.

❀ *Baked Creamed Mushrooms*

TO SERVE 4

1 heaping tablespoon of butter
1 tablespoon of flour
2 cups of milk, scalded
1 1/2 pounds of button mushrooms, whole, or larger ones,
    quartered
4 pimientos, drained and minced
1/8 teaspoon of cayenne pepper or 1 teaspoon of prepared
    mustard
2 cups of heavy cream, at room temperature
1/2 cup of bread crumbs
Salt

In the top of a double boiler, blend butter and flour. Put directly over a low flame and slowly add scalded milk, stirring carefully until thick. Assemble double boiler, add mushrooms, salt, cover, and cook for 10 minutes. Uncover. Add cayenne and half the pimiento and stir well. Add cream and stir again. Pour into a buttered casserole dish, cover with bread crumbs, dot with remaining pimiento, and bake in a 325° oven for 20 minutes.

❀ *Baked Deviled Mushrooms*

A tossed salad or hot buttered rice and green peas make fitting accompaniments.

TO SERVE 4

16 large mushrooms
1/2 cup of rich stock
2 tablespoons of butter
1 cup of bread crumbs
1/4 teaspoon of dry mustard
1/4 cup of minced pimiento
1/4 cup of minced olives
1/8 cup of pickled capers or nasturium seeds
Salt
1/8 teaspoon of cayenne pepper

Remove mushroom stems and insides and mince these fine. Lay mushroom caps, top down, in a shallow baking pan or casserole and pour stock around them. Simmer very slowly over a low flame for 5 minutes. Meanwhile, sauté stems and insides in butter in a skillet for 5 minutes, and then mix in bread crumbs and all other ingredients, moistening mixture with a little of the stock. Fill mushroom caps and bake, covered, for 10 minutes in a 350° oven.

✿ Baked Stuffed Mushrooms, Country Style

TO SERVE 4

16 large mushrooms (the larger the better)
12 green olives, minced
1 cup of well-seasoned stock
Salt and pepper
3 tablespoons of butter
1 cup of bread crumbs

Remove stems and insides of mushrooms, putting caps aside. Mince these with olives and cook slowly in a saucepan with 1/2 cup of stock for 5 minutes. Salt and pepper and add 2 tablespoons of butter. When butter has melted, add bread crumbs to make a paste. With this mixture fill the mushroom caps. Lay caps, filled side up, in a baking pan containing the remaining stock. Dot with remaining butter. Bake in a 350° oven for 20 minutes.

✿ Stuffed Mushrooms Baked in Cream

TO SERVE 4

16 large mushrooms
1 onion
3 tablespoons of butter
Salt
Touch of nutmeg
1 cup of light cream
4 slices of toast

Remove mushroom stems and scoop out insides. Chop these and onion thoroughly. With this mixture, fill mushroom caps and dot with butter. Sprinkle with salt and nutmeg. Lay mushrooms in a casserole or baking pan, add the cream, and bake 20 minutes in a 350° oven. Serve on toast, spooning cream over the mushrooms.

✿ Baked Mushrooms Stuffed with Ground Beef

TO SERVE 4

16 large mushrooms
3 tablespoons of minced parsley
1 tablespoon of minced pimiento
1 pound of ground beef
Pinch of sweet marjoram
Salt
1/8 teaspoon of pepper
1 cup of well-seasoned stock
1/4 cup of bread crumbs

Remove insides and stems of mushrooms, mince, and mix with parsley and pimiento. Add this mixture and the seasonings to the ground beef. Fill mushroom caps with the meat mixture. Set mushrooms in a baking pan, stuffed side up and half-deep in stock, moistening the meat filling with a little of the stock. Sprinkle with crumbs, bake 45 minutes in a 325° oven.

TO SERVE 4

16 large mushrooms
1/2 cup of leftover tongue, minced
1/2 cup of leftover chicken, minced
1/2 cup of bread crumbs
2 tablespoons of minced parsley
1/8 teaspoon of dry mustard
1/4 cup of cream
1 cup of well-seasoned stock

Remove the insides and stems of the mushrooms, mince, and mix with tongue, chicken, crumbs, parsley, and mustard. Moisten mixture with cream and 1/2 cup of stock. Fill mushroom caps with the mixture. Set mushrooms in a pan, stuffed side up and half-deep in stock, and bake for 20 minutes in a 350° oven.

❋ Baked Mushrooms Stuffed with Minced Ham and Rice

TO SERVE 4

1 cup of raw rice
Salt
2 tablespoons of butter
2 cups of rich meat stock
2 cups of minced pre-cooked ham, lean as possible
1 egg, well beaten
1 tablespoon of minced parsley
Touch of nutmeg
16 large mushroom caps. (Reserve stems for other uses.) *

Parboil rice in salted water for 15 minutes. Drain well. Butter a casserole and pour rice into this, leveling it out. Cover with 1 cup of stock. Combine minced ham thoroughly with egg, parsley, and nutmeg. Fill mushroom caps. Place on the rice, dot with butter, and pour over the remaining stock. Bake in a 350° oven for 30 minutes.

* Recipes which call for mushroom stems only are on pages 22, 23, 32, 39, 40, 41, 80, 81, 88, 94, 105, 112, 119, and 120.

❀ Baked Mushrooms in Cream

This dish can well be served with just plain buttered noodles or rice.

TO SERVE 4

1 1/2 pounds of large mushrooms
1 cup of milk
1/4 cup of heavy cream
1/4 cup of light cream
Salt
1/2 cup of bread crumbs
1 tablespoon of butter
4 pimientos, sliced

Slice mushrooms very thin from top to bottom, including stems. In a deep casserole, mix mushrooms with milk and creams and salt. Top with bread crumbs, dot with butter, and crisscross with pimiento slices. Bake, uncovered, in a 350° oven for 20 minutes.

❊ Baked Mushrooms in Wine

TO SERVE 6

1 1/2 pounds of mushrooms, sliced thin
2 tablespoons of butter
Salt and pepper
1/8 teaspoon of powdered nutmeg
1 cup of sauterne
8 to 10 thin baking powder biscuits, unbaked

In a saucepan sauté mushrooms gently in butter for 15 minutes. Pour into a casserole, season, and stir well. Pour in wine and stir well again. Top with biscuits and bake in a 350° oven until biscuits are brown.

❊ Mushrooms Baked in Ramekins

TO SERVE 4

2 tablespoons of butter
1 pound of mushrooms, sliced thin
Salt and pepper
1/2 cup of heavy cream, scalded
1/2 cup of milk, scalded
Pinch of nutmeg for each ramekin

In a skillet, melt butter, add mushrooms, salt, and pepper, and cook 15 minutes over a high flame. Toss several times. Divide into equal portions and fill 4 oven-proof ramekins. Pour into each equal amounts of cream and milk, sprinkle with nutmeg, and bake in a 350° oven for 10 minutes.

❀ Mushrooms with Marinara Sauce

Marinara is an Italian word which means "in the manner of sailors or fisherfolk" and, hence, "simple." And this is a simple and inexpensive dish which can well be served with plain boiled rice or spaghetti.

TO SERVE 4

1 clove of garlic, cut into quarters
1 medium-size onion, sliced thin in the round
2 tablespoons of olive oil or butter or margarine
1 #2 can (2 1/2 cups) of tomatoes
Salt and pepper
Touch of oregano or thyme
1 1/2 pounds of mushrooms, sliced thin

In a skillet, soften garlic and onion in the oil but do not brown. Put in tomatoes, seasonings, and oregano and cook slowly over a medium flame until the tomato pulp has broken down. Add mushrooms and cook slowly for 15 minutes more.

✿ *Scalloped Mushrooms*

TO SERVE 6

1 1/2 pounds of button mushrooms, whole
Salt
1/2 cup of stock
1 level tablespoon of flour
2 tablespoons of butter
1/2 cup of heavy cream
1/2 cup of light cream
1 teaspoon of powdered mustard
1 cup of grated cheese—parmesan preferably

Salt mushrooms and put them in an oven-proof casserole. Add stock and cook gently atop the stove over a low flame for 15 minutes. Meanwhile, blend flour and butter in a saucepan over a low flame and slowly add cream. When mixture is fairly thick, work in mustard and cheese. Pour over mushrooms and mix well. Place casserole under the broiler for 2 to 3 minutes or until the top is browned.

❁ *Scalloped Mushrooms with Leftover Meat*

This recipe makes use of leftover chicken, but tongue, ham, or veal will do nicely.

TO SERVE 6

1 pound of mushrooms, sliced thin
1 cup of clear stock
Pinch of powdered nutmeg
Pinch of powdered mace
Salt
1/2 cup of light cream, scalded
1/2 cup of milk, scalded
12 green olives, minced
12 black olives, minced
1/4 cup of dry sherry
1 cup of bread crumbs
2 cups of leftover chicken, julienned
1 tablespoon of minced pimiento

In a large saucepan, put mushrooms, stock, seasonings, and cream. Boil scalded milk for 10 minutes. Put mixture into a casserole and stir in olives, chicken, then the sherry. Cover with bread crumbs and bake for 15 minutes in a 350° oven. Remove from oven, top with pimiento, and serve.

❀ *Creamed Mushrooms on Toast*

TO SERVE 4

1 1/2 pounds of button mushrooms, whole, or larger mushrooms, quartered
1 cup of clear stock, beef or chicken
1 tablespoon of butter
1 tablespoon of flour
1 cup of light cream
Touch of powdered nutmeg
Salt and pepper
4 slices of dry toast

In a saucepan, boil mushrooms for 15 minutes in the stock. Drain, reserving the stock. Meanwhile, blend butter and flour over a low flame in another saucepan. Gradually pour in cream, stirring constantly to keep the sauce smooth. If too thick, add some of the stock. When you have the desired consistency (some like it thicker than others), put in mushrooms and seasonings. Bring to a bubble and pour over toast slices.

Variation

An interesting change can be rung on this basic creamed mushroom dish. Do *not* parboil mushrooms. *Omit* cream and nutmeg. Blend 1 level teaspoon of brown sugar with flour and butter and add stock (a bouillon cube dissolved in boiling water will do), *omitting* cream. Add mushrooms, reduce flame considerably, place saucepan over an asbestos pad, and simmer 20 minutes.

❀ *Mock Oysters*

TO SERVE 6

1 1/2 pound of small mushrooms, whole
1/2 cup of rich stock
1 cup of whole or skim milk
1 tablespoon of flour
3 tablespoons of butter
1/8 teaspoon of powdered nutmeg
1/8 teaspoon of cayenne pepper
1 tablespoon of onion juice
Salt
6 slices of dry toast

In a saucepan, boil mushrooms in stock for 10 minutes, un-covered, to permit most of liquid to evaporate. Meanwhile, in another saucepan, carefully mix milk and flour, stirring constantly to keep smooth. Pour this over mushrooms, add butter, and cook until thickened. Add all seasonings, stir well, and serve on toast.

Variation
After adding seasonings, remove from fire, add yolks of 2 eggs, stir gently, and serve.

✿ Mushrooms in Pattie Shells

With a tossed green salad, this makes a delightful dinner. Or serve with fresh green peas.

TO SERVE 4

6 slices of lean bacon (Canadian is best) or 1 cup of diced
    ham or pork
3 small onions, sliced very thin in the round and then
    quartered
1 tablespoon of flour
1/2 cup of dry white wine
1/8 teaspoon of nutmeg
A bouquet garni, made of several whole cloves and 1
    teaspoon of sweet basil, tied up in a small cheesecloth
    bag
1 1/2 pounds of mushrooms, chopped fine
2 cloves of garlic, crushed to a pulp
1 tablespoon of tomato paste
4 pattie shells

Chop bacon. In a skillet, brown bacon or other meat with onions. Remove. In remaining fat, mix flour, add wine, and stir constantly to keep mixture smooth. Put in the bouquet garni and cook several minutes, covered. Remove cover and garni and add mushrooms. Simmer slowly, uncovered, for about 10 minutes. Return onions and meat. Add tomato paste, garlic, and nutmeg, stirring carefully. When well blended, fill heated pattie shells with this mixture.

Note
You can, of course, fill pattie shells with one of several recipes given elsewhere in this book, such as on pages 22, 23, 76, and 79.

✿ *Mushroom Supreme*

This might be called a stew for it has everything: calories—
but not too many; vitamins and minerals—plenty of them; and
not too much but just enough fat.

TO SERVE 4

1 1/2 pounds of button mushrooms
2 tablespoons of butter
3 teaspoons of flour
1 cup of milk, scalded
2 dozen green olives, whole and not pitted
2 dozen black olives, whole and not pitted
2 tablespoons of capers, salted but washed
4 tablespoons of minced pimiento
2 cups of light cream
Salt and pepper
1 tablespoon of cognac or brandy (optional)
4 slices of dry toast

In a saucepan, boil mushrooms for 10 minutes in a small quantity of water or stock. In another saucepan, blend butter and
flour and gradually pour on scalded milk. Simmer slowly
over a low flame for 5 minutes. To this add olives, capers, and
pimientos and bring to a boil. Slowly add cream and stir well.
Add mushrooms and cook 5 minutes over a low flame. Season
to taste and stir in cognac if you wish. Serve on toast.

❀ *Mushroom and Vegetable Potpourri*

You may decide to serve this in soup plates with croutons or toast rounds.

TO SERVE 8

3 heaping tablespoons of butter
1 large onion, diced
6 ribs of celery, diced
3 small carrots, diced
2 green peppers, seeds removed, cut small
1 #2 can (2 1/2 cups) of hard-pack tomatoes
1/2 teaspoon of oregano or thyme
Salt and pepper
1/2 cup of stock
1 medium-size eggplant, pared and cubed
1 pound of small mushrooms, whole

In a deep saucepan, melt butter. Soften onion and then add all ingredients *except* eggplant and mushrooms. Cover and simmer for 15 minutes. Add eggplant and cook uncovered for 10 minutes. Now add mushrooms and cook briskly for 10 minutes more, uncovered.

❀ Mushroom, Meat, and Vegetable Stew

TO SERVE 6

2 tablespoons of any vegetable fat
1 pound of fresh mushrooms, sliced, or 1/4 pound of
    dried mushrooms (see page 10), shredded
1 pound of top sirloin, cubed small
1/2 cup of celery, diced
1/2 cup of carrots, diced
1/2 cup of fresh peas, plus a few of their pods
1/2 cup of string beans, cut small
1 or 2 cabbage leaves, shredded fine
1/8 teaspoon of nutmeg
Salt and pepper
2 tablespoons of whole unsalted almonds (optional)

In a deep skillet, bring fat to a high heat. In this braise mushrooms quickly. Remove them and then braise the meat, taking
care not to overbrown it. Add vegetables and seasonings, cover,
and cook very slowly for 30 minutes. Uncover, add the mushrooms, stir in almonds, and serve.

❀ *Mushroom Short Cake*

TO SERVE 4

1/2 cup of milk
1 tablespoon of Worcestershire sauce or 1 bouillon cube
2 tablespoons of butter
1 teaspoon of flour
1 pound of mushrooms, sliced very thin
1/2 cup of heavy cream
1/8 teaspoon of cayenne pepper or dry mustard
4 baking powder biscuits

In a double boiler, scald milk and add Worcestershire sauce (or dissolve bouillon cube). In a saucepan, blend butter and flour over a low flame. Slowly pour on the milk, stirring constantly until mixture thickens. Add mushrooms and cook over very low flame for 10 minutes. Add heavy cream and stir well. Cook 5 minutes longer. Season and pour over hot biscuits.

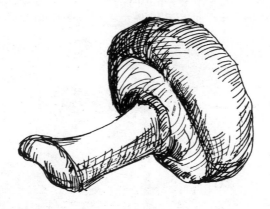

❀ *Mushroom Fritters*

Serve this hot—with or without a white sauce.

TO SERVE 6

1/2 tablespoon of butter
1 1/2 cups of mushroom stems, chopped fine
A batter made with:
      1/2 cup of sifted flour
      1/2 teaspoon of baking powder
      1 egg, well-beaten
      1/2 cup of milk
      Salt
   mixed well to a consistency heavier than cream
Fat for deep frying

In a skillet, melt butter and sauté mushrooms for 10 minutes over a low flame. Cool and then mix with batter. In an appropriate kettle for deep frying, heat fat to 325°. When at proper temperature, drop in the mushroom batter, a tablespoon at a time, and fry until golden brown. Drain well on brown paper.

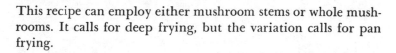 **Mushroom and Potato Fritters**

This recipe can employ either mushroom stems or whole mushrooms. It calls for deep frying, but the variation calls for pan
frying.

TO   SERVE   8

1 cup of minced mushroom stems, salted and peppered
3 cups of unbuttered mashed potatoes, combined with a
    touch of nutmeg
1/2 cup of grated cheese
1/2 cup of milk, scalded
1 tablespoon of flour
Bread crumbs
2 to 3 eggs, well beaten
Fat for deep frying

In a saucepan, combine mushrooms, potatoes, and cheese and
mix thoroughly. Add milk and cook over a low flame for 10
minutes, stirring constantly. Quickly work in flour and allow
mixture to cool. When well cooled, form into balls, patties, or
sticks, roll in crumbs, dip in egg, roll in crumbs again, and set
out to dry—about 10 minutes. In a suitable kettle, bring fat to
deep frying temperature, about 375°, drop in mushroom mixture, and remove as soon as each begins to brown. Drain on
brown paper and serve.

Variation

If you prefer a kind of pancake to the fritters, omit egg, and
spoon mixture into a greased frying pan, browning each cake
on both sides.

❀ Mushroom and Meat Ball Pie

TO SERVE 4

*Pastry dough, enough to line and cover an 8 x 8 x 2 cake
    pan or casserole*
1/2 pound of chopped beef
1 tablespoon of minced parsley
1 egg, well beaten
1/4 cup of bread crumbs
1 teaspoon of flour
1 cup of well-seasoned stock
1 1/4 pounds of small mushrooms
Salt and pepper

Line the pan with half the dough, and brown for 10 minutes
in a 325° oven. Make very small meat balls of the meat, parsley,
egg, and bread crumbs. Thicken the stock with the flour and
season. Cook the meat balls in the stock in a saucepan for 25
minutes on top of the stove. Add the mushrooms, pour the
mixture into the cake pan and cover with remaining pastry
dough. Ventilate with gashes. Bake for 20 minutes in a 325°
oven.

✺ Mushrooms and Veal

For a delectable dinner, serve this with plain buttered rice and green peas.

TO SERVE 6

1 medium-size onion, minced to a pulp
1 clove of garlic, mashed well
3 tablespoons of olive oil, butter, or margarine
1 pound of lean veal, cut up into knuckle-size pieces
Salt and pepper
1 pound of button mushrooms, whole, or large mush-
    rooms, quartered
2 bay leaves
8 whole cloves
1/2 cup of dry sherry or sauterne
Juice of 1/2 lemon

In a skillet, soften onion and garlic in oil slowly. In this, sauté veal pieces gently for 20 minutes, turning constantly. Add salt, pepper, and mushrooms. Cook, uncovered, for 10 minutes over a low flame. Now add bay leaves and cloves. Raise flame and add the wine. When at a boil, shut off flame, and briskly stir in the lemon juice.

❀ *Mushrooms and Veal Scaloppine*

Scaloppine simply means "small pieces."

TO SERVE 6

2 pounds of veal scaloppine, wafer thin
1 tablespoon of flour
Salt
3 tablespoons of butter
1 cup of well-seasoned stock (a bouillon cube will do)
1/2 pound of mushrooms, sliced thin
1/2 cup of marsala, madeira, sherry, or sauterne

Lightly flour and salt veal scaloppine. In a skillet, melt butter and in this sauté the meat. When pieces are brown, add stock and mushrooms gradually. Bring to a boil, then lower flame, cover, and cook for 20 minutes. Turn meat at least once during this time. (If flour begins to lump, stir gravy vigorously until it is smooth.) Add wine, bring to a boil, and serve.

Variation

A variation of the above recipe omits wine and adds green peppers. Slice 3 green peppers lengthwise and cook slowly for 10 minutes, covered. Mix with meat before adding stock.

TO SERVE 4

8 medium-size mushrooms
8 loin lamb chops, with fat trimmed off, to weigh about
    3 pounds
1 1/2 tablespoons of butter
1/8 teaspoon of nutmeg
1/2 tablespoon of minced chervil (finely minced young
    scallions will do)
Salt and pepper
1/4 cup of sherry

Remove stems from mushrooms and chop stems finely. Wrap the tail of each lamb chop around a mushroom cap, keeping it in place with a small skewer or toothpick. Melt 1/2 table-spoon of butter and brush chops and mushrooms with this, sprinkling nutmeg on the mushrooms. Broil 10 minutes on one side and 8 minutes on the other.

Meanwhile, melt remaining butter in a small saucepan, add mushroom stems, minced chervil, salt, and pepper. Sauté for 10 minutes over a low flame. Increase flame considerably and cook for 5 minutes or until liquid in pan has appreciably evaporated. Now add the sherry and cook *slowly* for 3 minutes. Place chops on a hot platter and pour over the mushroom sauce.

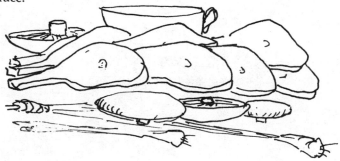

TO SERVE 4

3 tablespoons of butter
1 onion, minced to a pulp
1 clove of garlic, minced fine
8 loin lamb chops, all fat trimmed off, rolled and tied, to
    weigh about 3 pounds
1 #2 can (2 1/2 cups) of tomato purée
Pinch of oregano or thyme
Salt and pepper
18 medium-size mushrooms

In a casserole or in a skillet, melt butter and in it soften onion
and garlic over a low flame—about 10 minutes. In this, brown
chops—8 minutes to a side. Gradually add tomato purée and
all seasonings. After a fast initial boil, allow to simmer for 15
minutes. Add mushrooms, whole, and cook an additional 10
minutes at a slow bubbling boil.

TO SERVE 4

1 large beef kidney or 12 lamb kidneys
1/2 cup of dry white wine or 1/4 cup of wine vinegar
3 tablespoons of olive oil or melted butter
1 large onion, sliced thin in the round
1/8 teaspoon of oregano or thyme
Salt and pepper
1 pound of mushrooms, sliced thin

Cut kidney into small pieces and soak in water for 1 hour. Drain and dry. Marinate in 1/4 cup of wine for 1 hour. In a skillet, heat olive oil and onion together for 5 minutes over a low flame. Add kidneys with the marinade, oregano, salt, and pepper. Cover and cook slowly for 15 minutes. Remove cover, raise flame, and cook until liquid is appreciably reduced. Now add the sliced mushrooms, and reduce the flame; cook for 10 minutes or until the liquid has cooked long enough to have been reduced a second time; pour in the remainder of the wine, heat, and serve.

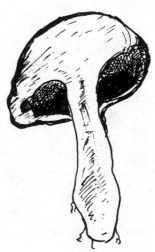

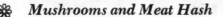 Mushrooms and Meat Hash

This is an excellent way of using up leftover mushroom stems. If in place of the lamb called for here you have a leftover piece of lean beef, veal, or chicken, by all means use that. Lamb has been given here simply because it seems to be the most difficult leftover meat to dispose of.

TO SERVE 4

2 cups of leftover lamb, free of all fat and diced small
2 cups of fresh mushroom stems, sautéed or boiled for 15
minutes, or 2 ounces of dried mushrooms (see page
10), cut up small
1 tablespoon of minced black olives
1 tablespoon of minced green olives
1 tablespoon of minced pimiento
1/2 cup of milk
1 tablespoon of butter
4 eggs, well beaten
1 teaspoon of powdered ginger
Salt and pepper

Place lamb, mushrooms, olives, and pimiento in a deep skillet with milk and butter. Heat slowly. When liquid is hot but *not* boiling, add the eggs and seasonings. Let cook slowly for about 5 minutes over a low flame. When eggs begin to harden fold them into the mixture. Serve when the eggs are of the consistency that you like best.

✤ *Mushrooms and Ham*

TO SERVE 4

1 pound of precooked smoked ham, cubed small
1 pound of mushrooms, sliced
2 tablespoons of sherry or any sweet white wine
1/8 teaspoon of powdered nutmeg
4 slices of toast

Trim fat from ham and render ham in a skillet, pouring off any fat. Add mushrooms, cook 10 minutes over a slow fire, stirring constantly. When mushrooms take on color, add wine and nutmeg. Serve over toast.

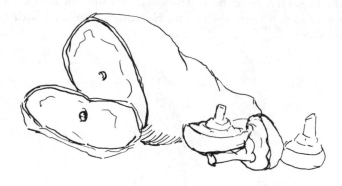

TO SERVE 6

2 tablespoons of butter
2 tablespoons of brown sugar
1 teaspoon of flour
1 pound of mushrooms, sliced thick
1/8 teaspoon of mace
1/8 teaspoon of nutmeg
6 thin slices of precooked ham—boiled or baked
1/4 cup of sweet sherry

In a large skillet, melt butter but do not brown. Mix sugar and flour and blend into butter, keeping flame low. Add mushrooms and seasonings, cover pan, and—with flame still low—cook 5 minutes. Remove cover and lay ham slices over mushrooms. Raise flame slightly and allow ham to heat through. Pour in sherry, bring to a brisk boil, and shut off flame. Serve on a heated platter so that mushrooms are covered with the ham slices.

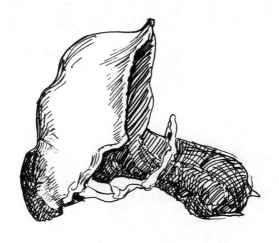

❄ *Ham Rolls with Mushroom Filling*

Dried mushrooms do especially well in this recipe. If you will serve 2 rolls per person, on a bed of plain boiled rice, the comments will be as satisfying as the dish.

TO SERVE 4

1/4 pound of dried mushrooms (see page 10), or 1 pound
of large mushrooms, sliced thin
8 slices of ham—baked Virginia, boiled, Prosciutto, or
Parma—sliced thin enough to be rolled and thick
enough to remain firm when rolled
1 small onion, minced
2 thin slices from a clove of garlic (optional)
1/4 cup of sweet white wine—sherry, marsala, or sauterne
1/4 teaspoon of powdered nutmeg

Trim outside fat from ham, dice fat, and render it slowly in a skillet with the onion and the garlic—20 minutes. Remove renderings, onion, and garlic, leaving fat in skillet. Drain mushrooms and dry. Slice very thin. Sauté mushrooms for 5 minutes in the fat over a fairly high flame. Remove mushrooms, taking care to have them as free of fat as possible, and spread over ham slices in equal proportions. Roll ham slices, tie with string, and lay in the skillet. Pour over the wine, season with nutmeg, and serve when ham has been heated through.

❊ *Mushrooms and Pork Tenderloin, Chinese Style*

This is best when served over boiled rice (1 cup of raw rice
will do) .

TO SERVE 4

1 tablespoon of olive oil or butter
1 clove of garlic, mashed well
1 small onion, minced to a pulp
1 pound of pork tenderloin, sliced very thin
1 tablespoon of soybean sauce
1 pound of mushrooms, sliced wafer thin
1/8 teaspoon of powdered mace

In a large skillet, heat oil and in this soften garlic and onion
but do not burn. In the oil sauté the tenderloin slices for 20
minutes—very slowly. Stir in soybean sauce, raise flames somewhat, and spread mushrooms over the meat. Cover the skillet
and allow to cook 15 minutes. Uncover, raise flame to allow
some evaporation, add mace, and cook 2 to 3 minutes more—
very rapidly.

✤ Mushrooms and Pork Chips

TO SERVE 4

1 tablespoon of butter
1 small clove of garlic, sliced very thin
1 pound of pork tenderloin or lean pork, sliced very
 thin and then diced
1 pound of fresh mushrooms, whole, or 1/4 pound of
 dried mushrooms (see page 10), sliced
1/8 teaspoon of powdered nutmeg
1/8 teaspoon of powdered ginger
1/8 teaspoon of cayenne pepper
Salt
1/2 cup of dry white wine

In a skillet, melt butter and soften garlic. In this, over a high flame, brown pork chips, stirring constantly. Add seasonings, then cover, lower flame, and cook slowly for 30 minutes. Add mushrooms and cook, uncovered, for several minutes more. Add the wine, raise flame, and cook 5 minutes before serving.

This is a stuffing or filling that can be used in a variety of ways. One, of course, is as a stuffing for small fowl (chicken, quail, pigeon, squab, or Cornish hen) or for a small rooster. Another is with egg rolls—if you know how to make egg rolls. Or with blintzes—if you know how to make blintzes. Or with ravioli or canelloni—if you know how to make them. Cooks adept at making pastry shells or persons near enough to a bakery that sells pattie shells can find another use for the filling.

One word of caution: This is a basic recipe. You will want to modify it by adding shredded meat or fish for patties or, perhaps, a small amount of vegetables. You may wish to add chopped nuts or pimiento or capers. But *NEVER* add anything in such quantity as to overpower the mushrooms.

MAKES ABOUT 3 CUPS

3 tablespoons of butter

1 small onion or several shallots, minced fine

1/2 pound of mushrooms or the stems of a little more than a pound of mushrooms—in either case, chopped fine

1/2 cup of well-seasoned meat or poultry stock. (Fish stock will do if you are adding shredded fish to make a pattie filling.)

1 cup of fine bread crumbs

Salt

Goodly dash of cayenne pepper

1 egg, well-beaten

In a skillet, melt butter and sauté onions and mushrooms for 5 minutes but never allow the butter to become very hot. Add the stock gradually, increase flame slightly, and allow to simmer 3 minutes. Now shut off the flame, add bread crumbs, and stir thoroughly. Season at this point. Just before mixture becomes cool, add egg, folding in with great care and thoroughness to avoid having egg cook. (It is merely a binder and will cook when the mixture is placed in the fowl, egg rolls, or ravioli.)

If you are stuffing a roasting fowl, surround the bird with a quantity of mushrooms, whole or sliced, and let them cook in the juices.

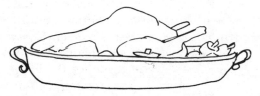

❀ *Mushrooms and Breast of Chicken I*

TO SERVE 4

Breasts of 2 roasting chickens or of 4 fryers, without skin
4 eggs
1 cup of fine bread crumbs
1/2 cup of butter or margarine
6 large mushrooms, thinly sliced
6 thin slices of cheese—parmesan, gruyère, muenster, or
(if you must) American
1/2 cup of rich chicken broth
Juice of 1 lemon
Salt

Cut breasts into thin slices. Beat eggs well and salt to taste. Immerse chicken slices in eggs for 1 hour. Then roll gently in bread crumbs.

In a casserole, heat butter but do not brown. Fry chicken slices in the butter, turning when golden brown on one side. Cover with the mushrooms and over the mushrooms lay the slices of cheese. Put casserole in a moderate 350° oven and cook 30 minutes, basting occasionally with the stock. Before taking to the table, squeeze lemon juice over the chicken to your taste.

95

TO SERVE 4

4 tablespoons of pork lard, diced
Breasts of 2 roasting chickens or of 4 fryers, skinned
1 pound of button mushrooms, boiled in a small quantity
     of stock for 15 minutes and then drained well, or 2
     cans of button mushrooms, drained, or 1/4 pound of
     dried mushrooms (see page 10)
12 very small onions
Salt and pepper
1 tablespoon of flour
1/4 cup of sherry

In a casserole or skillet atop the stove, render pork lard. Remove or not as you please. In the rendered lard, brown chicken breasts. Cover, and cook over a low flame for 15 minutes. Add mushrooms, onions, salt, and pepper. Put flour in a cup and carefully stir in a small amount of liquid from the casserole. When smooth and runny, pour into casserole, stirring well. Add sherry, raise flame for 2 minutes, and serve.

❀ Mushrooms and Chicken alla Cacciatora

In Italian *alla cacciatora* means "according to the way hunters prepare it" or, more simply, "hunter's style." And all true *alla cacciatora* dishes are simple ones, employing wine, although in many Italian-American restaurants this type of cooking has become confused with the Creole, with the result that peppers and other vegetables are included.

TO SERVE 4

4 tablespoons of olive oil
1 large onion, sliced in the round
2 cloves of garlic, whole
1 cup of sliced mushrooms
5 pounds of chicken fryers or broilers, or a tender fowl
*   or roasting chicken*
1 cup of tomato purée or a #2 can (2 1/2 cups) of hard-
*   pack tomatoes*
1/2 cup of red wine
Salt and pepper

In a thick-bottomed skillet, heat olive oil. In this, brown onion, garlic, and mushrooms. Remove with a skimming ladle and set aside. Meanwhile, have chicken cut into small pieces (cut at the joints and then cut again) and dried. Brown chicken pieces in oil. Return onion, garlic, and mushrooms, adding tomato purée. Cook slowly, uncovered, for at least 45 minutes. Add wine, raise flame, cook 5 minutes more. Salt and pepper to taste and serve.

Variation

After removing onions, garlic, and mushrooms, soften in the oil 2 green peppers, sliced lengthwise into eighths. Remove peppers before browning chicken and return them when you return the mushrooms. Proceed as above.

❄ *Mushrooms and Fillets of Fish*

Another dish that is at its best when served over a bed of plain rice.

TO SERVE 4

1 clove of garlic, crushed
1 small onion, minced
3 tablespoons of olive oil
1/2 pound of mushrooms, thinly sliced
1 pound of the fillets of any dry fish—halibut, haddock, flounder, or sole. The fillets should be fairly thin
1 cup of any fish or vegetable stock. (You may remove stems of the mushrooms, boil them 10 minutes in just enough water to cover, and use this as stock.)
Salt and pepper
Cayenne pepper
1 heaping teaspoon of flour

In a skillet over a low flame, soften garlic and onion in the olive oil. Add sliced mushrooms and spread evenly over the skillet. Sauté without turning, covered, for 5 minutes. Uncover and let simmer very slowly until liquid is appreciably reduced. Spread fish fillets over mushrooms, cover with stock, and raise flame to a moderate height. Add salt, pepper, and cayenne. As the fillets cook, remove 1/2 cup of liquid with a spoon and blend with flour. Gradually pour back into pan, working gently under the fish. Cook 15 minutes and serve.

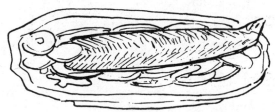

❋ Braised Mushrooms and Fish

Although this recipe is best when made with dried mushrooms, you can, of course, substitute fresh or canned ones.

TO SERVE 4

1/2 cup of minced ham, fat trimmed off
2 tablespoons of olive oil
1 clove of garlic, sliced fine
2 pounds of porgy, mullet, haddock, or mackerel
2 tablespoons of minced onion, leek, or scallion
1 tablespoon of minced chervil
2 ounces of dried mushrooms (see page 10), shredded
1/4 teaspoon of shredded ginger
1/8 teaspoon of cayenne pepper
1/4 cup of any white wine

In a skillet, heat ham, olive oil, and garlic. Braise fish in this at once, 5 minutes on each side. Add onions and chervil, cover, and simmer for 5 minutes. Now add mushrooms, ginger, cayenne, and wine. Cover again and cook 5 minutes more. Uncover, raise flame high for 2 minutes, and serve at once.

Increasing the quantity of ginger will give a sharper tang to this dish—if that is what you like.

TO SERVE 6

1 clove of garlic, crushed
1 tablespoon of butter (or any desired fat)
1/2 cup of minced onions
1 green pepper, sliced thin in long strips
2 ribs of celery, julienned
2 pounds of porgy (halved) or of shad, whitefish, or
    haddock (in small chunks)
1 pound of large mushrooms, sliced
Salt and pepper
1/2 cup of court bouillon or any clear stock
1/2 teaspoon of ginger, powdered or shredded
1/2 cup of blanched almonds (optional)
1/4 cup of sherry or any dried white wine (optional)

In a skillet, sauté garlic in butter. Then, 2 minutes apart, in this order, add: onions, green pepper, and celery and sauté gently over a low flame for 10 minutes after adding the celery. Now put in the fish and cook slowly for 10 minutes, turning fish over once—gently. Cover fish with mushroom slices and let simmer, covered, for 10 minutes without stirring or turning. Add stock, ginger, salt, and pepper and bring to a quick boil. At this point put in your almonds, shut off the flame, and add the wine.

Variation
Those who like a thick gravy may wish to add 1 tablespoon of flour or cornstarch to the stock. This should be blended in a cup, poured in slowly, and the mixture allowed time to cook away the floury taste.

❀ *Casserole of Mushrooms and Fillets of Fish*

TO SERVE 4

1 pound of mushrooms, sliced wafer thin
1/8 pound of butter
1 teaspoon of powdered ginger
1 tablespoon of flour
1 cup of light cream or milk
1 large onion, chopped fine
Salt
2 pounds of any fish fillet—say, haddock, flounder, sole,
*   red snapper, or mullet*
Dash of cognac (optional)

Lay mushroom slices in the bottom of a greased casserole. In a cup, cream butter, ginger, and flour and slowly stir in half the cream until you have a smooth, runny mixture. Pour over mushrooms and sprinkle with minced onion. Salt as desired. Over this lay fillets. Pour remaining cream over all and bake, uncovered, for 20 minutes in a 350° oven. Before serving, add dash of cognac.

❀ Mushrooms and Oysters

Served with a plain lettuce salad, this makes a delectable dish.

TO SERVE 4

16 large mushroom caps. (Reserve stems for other uses.) *
2 tablespoons of butter or olive oil
Salt
16 plump raw oysters, shelled
Cayenne pepper
1 cup of Béchamel Sauce or of Salsa Verde (page 31)
    heated in a double boiler

Place mushroom caps half-deep in a pan of boiling water. In each put a small chunk of butter and a sprinkling of salt. Broil for 3 to 5 minutes. Over each mushroom cap place an oyster with a sprinkling of cayenne. Return to broiler and broil 3 minutes. Top with sauce.

Béchamel Sauce
Consult any standard cook book or try this simple form:

1 cup of rich, well-seasoned meat stock
1 cup of cream, light or heavy
3 tablespoons of butter
1 1/2 tablespoons of flour
1 medium onion, grated
1 carrot, grated
6 whole peppercorns
Salt

In a saucepan, scald stock and cream and in it cook onions, carrots, and peppercorns over a very low flame to avoid boiling. In another saucepan, blend butter with flour. Strain first mixture, disposing of any hard ingredients, and slowly pour over butter and flour mixture. Heat thoroughly and salt to taste.

* Recipes which call for mushroom stems only are on pages 22, 23, 32, 39, 40, 41, 80, 81, 88, 94, 105, 112, 119, and 120.

❀ Mushrooms and Soft Shell Crabs

An interesting combination. The Chinese have an elaborate form that would tax the ordinary home. This is a simple dish to prepare and an easy one to eat. Serve it with a green vegetable.

TO SERVE 6

1 clove of garlic, crushed

2 onions, finely minced

2 tablespoons of olive oil or any desired fat

2 ribs of celery, diced small

3 leeks, finely minced

1 pound of large mushrooms, thinly sliced

1/8 teaspoon of turmeric or chili powder

1/8 teaspoon of powdered ginger

Salt and pepper

12 soft shell crabs

1/2 cup of well-seasoned fish stock or meat stock or bouillon

1/2 cup of dry sherry

In a broad skillet that will hold the 12 crabs side by side, sauté the garlic and onion in the oil until soft. Add celery and leeks, cover, and cook slowly for 10 to 15 minutes or until the vegetables yield some of their juices. Now introduce the mushrooms, cover, and cook 10 minutes or until some more liquid develops. Uncover, increase flame, and permit part of the liquid to evaporate. At this point add seasonings. Lay the crabs atop the mixture, adding wine and stock. Cover tightly and cook 10 minutes more. Serve immediately.

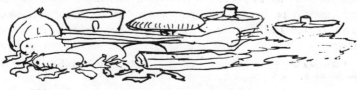

❀ Mushrooms and Conch

Conch may be had in the form of huge, flat clams, like abalone in California; or of spectacularly large twisted shells, found along the Florida coast; or of the small periwinkle snail, varying in size from a child's fist to a man's, found along the Eastern seaboard. Unless you do as follows, the meat is tough: (1) Boil shells for 1 hour in a saucepan, starting with cold water. (2) Remove meat from shells and slice or not as you please. (3) Cook the meat in a small amount of water in a saucepan for 1 to 1 1/2 hours. Or cook the meat in a pressure cooker under 15 pounds pressure for 20 to 30 minutes.

TO SERVE 6

1 clove of garlic, crushed

1/2 cup of minced onions

2 tablespoons of butter

1/2 cup of celery, diced small

Salt

3/4 pound of large mushrooms, sliced thin

1 cup of court bouillon or well-seasoned stock

Dash of powdered nutmeg

1/8 teaspoon of powdered ginger

Freshly ground black pepper

Meat of large conch or of 4 fair-size periwinkle ones—cut small, almost julienned

1/4 cup of sherry—the drier the better

In a large skillet over a fairly high flame, sauté garlic and onions in butter, covered. When soft, add celery and salt at this point. Cover with mushroom slices, reduce flame, and cook 5 minutes. Pour in stock and add remaining seasonings. Raise flame to evaporate considerable of the liquid. Now put in conch meat and, when it is hot, add wine. Cook 3 minutes and serve.

❊ *Mushroom Omelet*

One way of using mushroom stems.

TO SERVE 4

1 cup of mushroom stems, minced fine
1/2 cup of well-seasoned stock
2 tablespoons of butter
8 eggs
1/4 cup or less of light cream
Salt and pepper

Cook mushroom stems in stock for 15 minutes. In a large skillet melt butter. Meanwhile beat together eggs and cream, adding salt and pepper. Pour into skillet. Strain mushrooms, salting and peppering them. When eggs are firm, lay mushrooms over one half the omelet and fold the other half over. After several seconds, lift and turn omelet to brown for a few seconds on the other side. Serve immediately.

❊ Mushrooms and Poached Eggs

An excellent dish for a light luncheon or a summer supper, this mushroom dish with eggs is fortified by the addition of precooked ham and the use of nutmeg and sherry lifts it out of the ordinary run of light dishes for the menu.

TO SERVE 4

1 tablespoon of butter
6 tablespoons of minced ham, lean and precooked
1 cup of chicken stock
1/2 pound of large mushrooms, sliced wafer thin
3 tablespoons of sherry
8 eggs
Nutmeg

In a saucepan, melt butter and stir in ham and stock. Add mushrooms and cook 5 minutes over a high flame. When liquid has been considerably reduced, add sherry. Cook 10 minutes over a low flame. Now break in the eggs, cover, and cook until eggs are firm—about 6 minutes. Serve with a sprinkling of nutmeg.

TO SERVE 4

2 tablespoons of butter
1 small onion, minced
1 pound of mushrooms, sliced thin
2 cups of green peas, parboiled 10 minutes
4 eggs, well beaten
2 tablespoons of grated cheese—parmesan or Swiss
Salt and pepper
4 slices of dry toast

In a skillet, melt butter over a moderate flame and add onion. When onion has colored, add mushrooms and sauté over a low flame for 10 minutes. Raise flame and continue cooking until liquid has appreciably evaporated. Add peas and again reduce flame. Cook 5 minutes. Now mix in eggs and cook until eggs are almost hard. Add cheese, salt, and pepper. Raise flame for a second or so and stir vigorously. Serve on toast.

Variation

A simplified version of this dish calls for 8 eggs but *no cheese,* and can be garnished with cooked peas. Substitute 1 clove of minced garlic for the onion. Proceed as above until liquid has been reduced. Now stir in eggs, salt, and pepper, and stir until well scrambled.

TO SERVE 8

1 pound of button mushrooms, whole
1/2 cup of meat stock
1 pound of spaghetti or any other pasta
1 cup of pimientos, minced
1/2 cup of green olives, minced
1/2 cup of black olives, minced
3/4 cup of milk, scalded
Salt and pepper
1 cup of grated cheese, cheddar preferably
Paprika

Parboil the spaghetti 8 minutes (counting the time after the initial boil). Combine pimiento, olives, and milk with the mushrooms, making an even mixture over the bottom of the casserole. Over this lay the spaghetti (drained) mixed with the grated cheese. Sprinkle with paprika, and bake, uncovered, 20 to 25 minutes in a 350° oven.

Note

If you prefer solid to grated cheese, use 1/2 pound of cheddar, half of which is cubed and half sliced. Combine cubes with spaghetti and cover the top with the cheese slices. Bake for the same length of time.

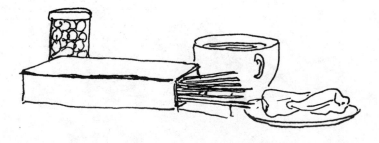

✻ *Mushrooms with Pasta*

TO SERVE 6

1 pound of narrow noodles
1 tablespoon of butter
1/2 cup of shredded cooked chicken
1/2 cup of sliced pimiento
1 pound of mushrooms, sliced wafer thin
2 cups of milk—whole, skimmed, or evaporated
1 cup of light cream
Salt

Parboil noodles 8 minutes in salted water and drain well. Butter the bottom and sides of a deep casserole. Lay in the noodles. Cover with shredded chicken, pimiento, and mushrooms—in that order. Scald milk and cream together and pour over. Add salt. Bake, uncovered, in a 325° oven for 30 minutes.

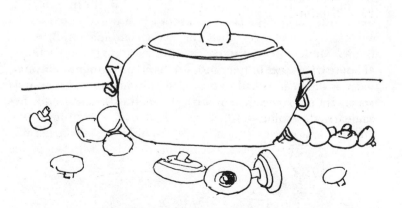

❈ *Timbale of Mushrooms and Pasta Shells*

While peas are called for here as the filling of the ring mold, naturally you will substitute any suitable vegetable of your preference.

TO SERVE 8

1 1/2 pounds of mushrooms, thinly sliced
1/2 cup of stock, very clear but seasoned
1 pound of pasta shells
Nutmeg
1 cup of grated cheese—parmesan or Swiss
1/2 cup of bread crumbs
2 tablespoons of butter
Salt
4 cups of cooked peas
1/2 cup of sliced pimiento

Boil mushrooms in stock for 5 minutes and drain thoroughly. Meanwhile parboil the pasta shells for 8 minutes in salted water and drain thoroughly. With the pasta combine mushrooms, nutmeg, and most of the cheese. Butter a ring mold with 1 tablespoon of the butter and fill with mushroom mixture. Cover with bread crumbs and dot with remaining cheese and butter. Set mold in a pan, pouring in boiling water to half the height of the mold, and bake in a 325° oven for 30 minutes. Unmold on a platter (the mixture will hold its shape) and fill the center with the peas, decorating the ring with strips of pimiento.

❀ *Timbale of Mushrooms with Sweetbreads and Pasta*

If you will unmold this timbale onto a hot platter and ring with fresh green peas, you will have a most attractive and appetizing entrée.

TO SERVE 8

4 tablespoons of butter
1 pound of nugget-type pasta—shells, elbow macaroni, tubettini—parboiled for 8 minutes in salted water
1/8 teaspoon of powdered mace
Salt and pepper
1 tablespoon of flour
1 cup of light cream and milk, combined
1 pound of mushrooms, quartered
1 pound of sweetbreads, boiled and cubed (see Note *below)*

Butter a deep mold. Melt in a saucepan 2 tablespoons of butter. Mix parboiled pasta with mace and pour into butter. Set aside over a pan of hot water to keep warm. In another saucepan over a low flame, melt remaining butter. Blend in flour, gradually adding milk and stirring constantly. When mixture is thick, add mushrooms and sweetbreads. Season with salt and pepper and simmer for 10 minutes. Mix with the pasta and pour the mixture into a mold. Set mold half-deep in a pan of boiling water. Bake in a 325° oven for 25 minutes. Unmold and serve.

Note
Soak sweetbreads in salted water for 20 minutes. Remove fibers and veins. Put in a saucepan, cover with boiling water, and add juice of 1 lemon. Cook for 20 minutes, uncovered. Strain and cool under running water. Let sweetbreads dry until hard before cubing.

Baked Lasagne with Mushroom Sauce

This is a 3-step recipe and, all told, requires 2 1/2 hours of preparation and cooking time.

TO SERVE 6

> 2 tablespoons of olive oil or a vegetable fat
> 1 clove of garlic, whole
> 1 large onion, sliced in the round
> 3 cups of mushroom stems, minced, or of whole mushrooms, cut small. Or 3 ounces of dried mushrooms (see page 10), or 3 #2 cans (2 1/2 cups in all) of button mushrooms
> 1 #3 can (4 cups) of hard-pack tomatoes
> 2 tablespoons of tomato paste with an equal amount of boiling water
> Salt and pepper
> 1 pound of lasagne
> 2 cups of grated cheese—parmesan, preferably

This is a 3-step recipe. First, make a sauce thus: In a deep saucepan, heat oil and in it brown garlic and onion. Remove or not as you wish. In the oil brown the mushrooms, remove, and put aside. To the oil add tomatoes and cook very slowly for 1 hour or until pulp has broken down completely. Add tomato paste mixed with water and cook 30 minutes longer. Return mushrooms to the sauce, season, and cook 15 minutes longer. The sauce is now ready.

Second: Boil lasagne in salted water for 8 minutes. Wash under running cold water and leave soaking in water.

Third: Cover the bottom of a baking dish with some of the sauce. Over this place a layer of drained lasagne. Cover this with sauce and sprinkle with cheese. Continue in this way until lasagne has been used, ending with a topping of sauce and cheese. Bake in a 350° oven for 30 minutes.

Casserole of Mushrooms and Rice

TO SERVE 4

1 pound of mushrooms, coarsley minced
1 small onion, chopped fine
2/3 cup of raw rice
2 1/2 cups of stock or boiling water
1 tablespoon of tomato paste and 1/4 cup of stock or water
3 tablespoons of bread crumbs
3 tablespoons of butter or margarine
Salt and pepper

In an oven-proof casserole atop the stove, slowly cook onions and mushrooms, properly salted, in 1 tablespoon of butter. Keep flame very low. Meanwhile parboil rice in stock, boiling rapidly, for 15 minutes, or until stock is practically absorbed. Butter sides of the casserole and in it mix rice with mushrooms and onion. Dissolve tomato paste in stock or water and work into mushroom mixture, using a wooden spoon to avoid breaking the rice kernels. Dot with remaining butter and sprinkle with bread crumbs. Bake for 20 minutes in a 350° oven.

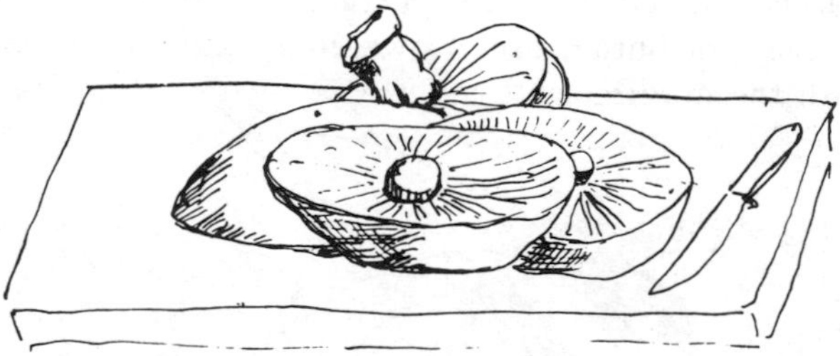

❀ Curried Mushrooms and Rice

Exotic, unusual, and quite, quite tasty, this is a variation of a well-known Indian dish.

TO SERVE 4

1 cup of raw rice

2 1/2 cups of seasoned stock

2 Bermuda or Italian onions, sliced very thin in the round

1 pound of button or small mushrooms

1 to 3 teaspoons of curry, depending on how much you like

2 large tomatoes, quartered

1/4 pound of butter, divided into 4 equal parts

Boil rice in stock for 30 minutes or until soft. While rice is boiling, slowly brown onion rings in 1 part of butter in a large skillet, covered, for 10 minutes. Uncover and push onions aside. Add another piece of butter and when it is melted add mushrooms. Cook slowly, uncovered, until brown—about 15 minutes. Push mushrooms against onions and add the third piece of butter, blending in the curry powder as the butter melts. In this gently color the tomato quarters—about 5 minutes. Drain rice. Place on a platter, making a crater in the center, and drop in last piece of butter. Fill this with tomato and onions and top with the mushrooms.

❀ Mushrooms and Broccoli

This is best when served over plain boiled rice.

TO SERVE 6

1 good-size bunch of broccoli, broken into natural seg-
ments, or 2 pounds of spinach or escarole
1 pound of small mushrooms, whole
2 tablespoons of butter
Dash of cayenne pepper
Salt and pepper
1/2 cup of chicken stock

Parboil broccoli for 10 minutes in minimum amount of boiling salted water. In a large skillet, sauté mushrooms in the butter, very gently, for 10 minutes. Drain broccoli and add to mushrooms. Sauté both another 10 minutes. Blend seasonings into the stock and add to mushrooms, stirring gently with a wooden spoon until well heated.

Variation

When you are blending seasonings into stock, add 1/2 teaspoon of anchovy paste or 6 anchovies, mashed.

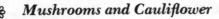

TO SERVE 8

1 head of cauliflower
1 pound of mushrooms
1 cup of clear stock
2 tablespoons of butter
2 cups of skim milk, hot
1/2 cup of bread crumbs
1/2 cup of blanched almonds (optional)
Salt and pepper

Stand cauliflower head down in cold, salted water for 1 hour. Then remove leaves and stalk and separate head into segments. In the stock, parboil the cauliflower very fast when it is properly seasoned, for 5 minutes. Butter a casserole with 1 tablespoon of butter and pour in cauliflower and mushrooms. Cover with milk, sprinkle with bread crumbs, dot with butter and almonds. Bake 20 minutes in a 350° oven.

❊ Mushrooms and Eggplant

Create an unusual color scheme on your table with this casserole. By itself it can be a one-dish meal for 4 persons or it can give zest to whatever other food you may be serving, such as plain buttered rice or spaghetti.

TO SERVE 6

1 medium-size eggplant, cut into 1-inch cubes, pared or not as you wish
1 pound of small mushrooms, whole, or of larger ones, quartered
2 tablespoons of tomato paste
Salt and pepper
4 tablespoons of olive oil or any other desired fat—butter, bacon drippings, rendered pork lard
1/2 cup of well-seasoned meat stock

In a large casserole, sauté together eggplant cubes, mushrooms, tomato paste, and seasonings in the oil or fat. After 5 minutes cover the skillet and let mixture cook 10 minutes. Uncover and cook until liquid has almost evaporated. Now add the stock and cook 5 minutes more, uncovered and very fast. Serve from the casserole.

❀ Mushrooms and Peppers

TO SERVE 4

> *3 tablespoons of olive oil or melted butter*
>
> *2 large green or red peppers, cleaned and sliced length-wise in eighths*
>
> *1 pound of button mushrooms, whole, or large ones, quartered*
>
> *Salt and pepper*

In a skillet, heat oil but not excessively. Sauté pepper slices for 5 minutes, covered, and 5 minutes, uncovered. When liquid has been considerably reduced, add mushrooms. Sauté, covered, for 15 minutes. Then uncover and cook until much of the liquid is evaporated. Salt and pepper to taste. Serve piping hot.

�֍ Green Peppers Stuffed with Mushrooms

This dish is a good one to make whenever you have leftover mushroom stems, but there is no reason why whole mushrooms cannot be used. Allow 1 pepper for each person and, with rice or pasta, you will have a complete meal. Serve hot or cold.

TO SERVE 4

4 large green peppers
4 cups of mushroom stems, coarsely cut, or of cut-up mushrooms
4 tablespoons of butter
4 slices of bread soaked in rich stock
Salt
Touch of cayenne pepper
2 onions, minced
A dozen or so green olives, minced
2 cups of rich stock

Parboil peppers for 5 minutes and let cool. Preserve stock in which they cooked. Cut off caps, one-half inch from top, and save. With a small spoon clean out pepper seeds and fibers, working carefully so as not to cut the walls. Set peppers aside.

In a skillet over a low flame, sauté mushrooms in butter. When they have colored, add the bread, squeezing out most of the stock and adding what you squeeze to the 2 cups of stock. After bread and mushrooms are thoroughly combined, add seasonings, onion, and olives. Lower flame, stir, and cook for 10 minutes.

Fill peppers with this mixture. If it seems too thick, add more stock. Place caps back on peppers and set them, half-deep in stock, in a baking pan. Bake for 20 minutes in a 350° oven.

Variation

Add a #2 can (2 1/2 cups) of hard-pack tomatoes, drained, with a small amount of thyme or oregano when adding bread. This makes a colorful filling.

❀ Tomatoes Stuffed with Mushrooms

This is another recipe making good use of mushroom stems.

TO   SERVE   4

4 large tomatoes
1 cup of finely minced mushroom stems or whole mush-
    rooms
1/2 clove of garlic, minced fine
1 1/2 tablespoons of butter
1 cup of rich stock
1/2 cup of fine bread crumbs
Salt and pepper

Cut around stem of tomato with a sharp knife, removing just enough of the top to allow room for a small spoon. Scoop out as much pulp as you can without bruising the walls of the tomato.

In a saucepan, cook mushrooms, tomato pulp, and garlic in 1 tablespoon of butter and 1/2 cup of stock until pulp has broken down somewhat—about 15 minutes. Season. Fill tomatoes with this mixture, top with bread crumbs, and dot with butter.

Place tomatoes in a baking pan, pour in remaining stock, and bake for 15 minutes in a 350° oven.

Variation

Substitute for the garlic 1 teaspoon of oregano or thyme. Cook mushrooms, tomato pulp, seasoning, and bread crumbs in butter for 5 minutes over a high flame, stirring constantly. Fill tomatoes and proceed as above, with oven at 400°.

❋ Scalloped Mushrooms and Potatoes

TO SERVE 6

*3 large potatoes, pared, sliced in rounds almost as thin as
   mushrooms*
*1 1/2 pounds of large mushrooms, sliced thin from top to
   bottom*
3 cups of skim milk—at room temperature
1 cup of seasoned stock—at room temperature
Touch of powdered nutmeg
Touch of powdered mace
Salt and pepper
1/2 cup of bread crumbs
1 tablespoon of minced pimiento
1 tablespoon of butter

Butter a casserole and put in a layer of potatoes and a layer of
mushrooms. Cover with combined milk and stock and sprinkle
with seasonings. Add another layer of potatoes and mushrooms
and proceed as above until all ingredients have been used. Top
with bread crumbs, dot with butter, and bake, covered for 40
minutes in a 350° oven. Sprinkle with pimiento before taking
casserole to table.

❀ Deep-dish Mushroom and Potato Pie

TO SERVE 6

1/4 cup of cubed ham, fat and all
1 pound of button or small mushrooms, whole
2 tablespoons of flour
3 to 4 cups of cold mashed potatoes
1/2 cup of milk, scalded
1 tablespoon of butter, melted

In a skillet, render ham and then gently sauté mushrooms. Butter sides and bottom of a casserole. Work 1 1/2 tablespoons of flour into potatoes and line sides and bottom of casserole, leaving enough for a topping. Mix 1/2 tablespoon of flour with mushrooms and then add milk. Pour into casserole, top with remaining potatoes, and brush with melted butter. Bake 20 to 25 minutes or until top is browned in a 325° oven.

❄ Mushrooms and Spinach, Oven-baked

This is indeed a first-class one-dish meal. Naturally, it can also be a side dish with such meat as scaloppine of veal. But it can stand alone superbly.

TO SERVE 4

2 pounds of spinach, boiled 2 minutes in only the water
    that clings to leaves after washing
3/4 pound of mushrooms, sliced thin
2 medium-size onions, minced to a pulp
2 tablespoons of butter
2 tablespoons of flour
3/4 cup of meat stock, or vegetable stock, or whole milk
Salt and pepper
Dash of powdered nutmeg
1/2 cup of bread crumbs

Place drained spinach in a buttered casserole. Keep casserole hot by placing it in a bath of boiling water. (Boiling water midway up in a baking pan will do the trick.)

In a skillet, sauté mushrooms and onions in butter, well heated but not browned. Turn constantly. This process should take 8 to 10 minutes. Work flour and stock into a smooth mixture and add to mushrooms. Cook until thickened, stirring all the while. Add seasonings. Lay the whole over the spinach and cover with bread crumbs. Bake for 20 minutes in a 350° oven. If necessary, brown crumbs under broiler flame.

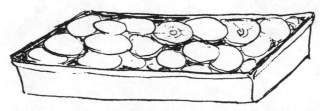

TO SERVE 4

1 pound of zucchini
2 peppers—preferably red
4 tablespoons of olive oil
2 cloves of garlic, crushed
1 onion, sliced in the round
1 #1 1/2 can (2 cups) of tomato purée and an equal
    amount of boiling water or stock
1/2 pound of mushrooms, sliced from top to bottom
1 tablespoon of oregano
Salt and pepper

Wash zucchini well and cut into rounds 2 inches long. Slice peppers lengthwise, 8 slices to a pepper. In a deep saucepan or skillet, heat oil and in it brown garlic and onion, but not too much. Add purée and boiling water. When this comes to a boil, add zucchini, peppers, and mushrooms. Cover and cook slowly for 20 minutes. Season during last 5 minutes. Serve piping hot.

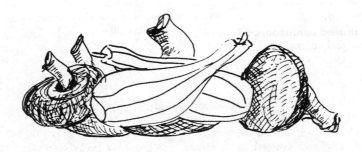

Mushroom stuffing:
for egg rolls, 94
for ham rolls, 91
for peppers, 119
for poultry, 94
for tomatoes, 120
Mushroom and vegetable potpourri, 77
Mushroom Vichysoisse, 35
Mushrooms: 5–19
under bell, 45
and beef, 49, 59, 65, 82, 88
and broccoli, 115
en brochette, 57
and cauliflower, 116
and chicken alla cacciatora, 97
and chicken breasts, 95, 96
and clams, 56
as a condiment, 25, 26, 27
and eggplant, 117
and eggs, 29, 49, 105, 106, 107
and fish, 98, 99, 100, 101
and ham, 67, 72, 89, 90, 91
and kidneys, 87
with lamb chops, 85, 86
with marinara sauce, 70
and meat hash, 88
and oysters, 102
with pasta, 109, 110, 111
in pattie shells, 75
and peppers, 58, 118, 119, 124
pickled, 27, 28
and pork chips, 93
and pork tenderloin, 92
and potatoes, 81, 121, 122
and·rice, 67, 113, 114
with Salsa Verde, 31
and soft shell crabs, 103
and spaghetti, 108
and spinach, 123
supreme, 76
and sweetbreads, 111
and tomatoes, 58, 61, 120
and tongue, 66, 72
and veal, 72, 83, 84
and vegetable potpourri, 77
and zucchini and peppers, 124
see also Baked mushrooms,
Broiled mushrooms, etc.

Nuts:
sautéed mushrooms with, 52
see also Chestnuts

Oil and mushroom sauce, 42
Onions:
and broiled mushrooms, 54
and skewered mushrooms, 57
Oyster and mushroom stew, 38
Oysters:
mock, 74
and mushrooms, 102

Pasta:
and mushrooms, 109, 110
and sweetbreads and mushrooms, 111
Pattie shells, mushroom filling for, 75, 94
Peppers:
and mushrooms in chicken alla cacciatora, 97
and mushrooms, sautéed, 118
and mushrooms on skewers, 57
mushroom stuffing for, 119
and mushrooms and zucchini, 124
Pickled mushroom salad, 30
Pickled mushrooms, 8, 14, 27, 30
Poisonous mushrooms, 6, 7–8
Pork chips and mushrooms, 93
Pork tenderloin and mushrooms, 92
Potato and mushroom fritters, 81
Potato and mushroom pie, 122
Potatoes and scalloped mushrooms, 121

Raw mushroom salad, 29
Rice:
and curried mushrooms, 114
and ham as mushroom stuffing, 67
and mushroom casserole, 113

Salad dressings:
Italian, 30
Salsa Verde, 31